theatre & museums

theatre &
museums

Susan Bennett

palgrave
macmillan

First published 2013 by
PALGRAVE MACMILLAN

Palgrave Macmillan in the UK is an imprint of Macmillan Publishers Limited, registered in England, company number 785998, of Houndmills, Basingstoke, Hampshire RG21 6XS.

Palgrave Macmillan in the US is a division of St Martin's Press LLC, 175 Fifth Avenue, New York, NY 10010.

Palgrave Macmillan is the global academic imprint of the above companies and has companies and representatives throughout the world.

Palgrave® and Macmillan® are registered trademarks in the United States, the United Kingdom, Europe and other countries

ISBN: 978–0–230–58020–6 paperback

This book is printed on paper suitable for recycling and made from fully managed and sustained forest sources. Logging, pulping and manufacturing processes are expected to conform to the environmental regulations of the country of origin.

A catalogue record for this book is available from the British Library.

Library of Congress Cataloging-in-Publication Data

Bennett, Susan, 1955–
    Theatre and museums / Susan Bennett.
        p. cm.
    Includes index.
    ISBN 978–0–230–58020–6
    1. Museum theater. 2. Performing arts in museums. I. Title.

AM7.B383 2013
069—dc23   2012032197

10   9   8   7   6   5   4   3   2   1
22 21 20 19 18 17 16 15 14 13

Printed in China

contents

series editors' preface

The theatre is everywhere, from entertainment districts to the fringes, from the rituals of government to the ceremony of the courtroom, from the spectacle of the sporting arena to the theatres of war. Across these many forms stretches a theatrical continuum through which cultures both assert and question themselves.

Theatre has been around for thousands of years, and the ways we study it have changed decisively. It's no longer enough to limit our attention to the canon of Western dramatic literature. Theatre has taken its place within a broad spectrum of performance, connecting it with the wider forces of ritual and revolt that thread through so many spheres of human culture. In turn, this has helped make connections across disciplines; over the past fifty years, theatre and performance have been deployed as key metaphors and practices with which to rethink gender, economics, war, language, the fine arts, culture and one's sense of self.

Theatre & is a long series of short books which hopes to capture the restless interdisciplinary energy of theatre and performance. Each book explores connections between theatre and some aspect of the wider world, asking how the theatre might illuminate the world and how the world might illuminate the theatre. Each book is written by a leading theatre scholar and represents the cutting edge of critical thinking in the discipline.

We have been mindful, however, that the philosophical and theoretical complexity of much contemporary academic writing can act as a barrier to a wider readership. A key aim for these books is that they should all be readable in one sitting by anyone with a curiosity about the subject. The books are challenging, pugnacious, visionary sometimes and, above all, clear. We hope you enjoy them.

Jen Harvie and Dan Rebellato

theatre & museums

What strange theater!
Paul Ardenne on Marina Abramović's 'The Artist Is
Present', Museum of Modern Art (MoMA), New York

The retrospective of Marina Abramović's forty-year career,
Marina Abramović: The Artist Is Present, at MoMA (14 March
to 31 May 2010) was at once performance, exhibition, and
archive. Evidence of four decades of production – traces
captured in videos, notes, objects, photographs – occupied
museum space along with 're-performances' of five of her
best-known works and a substantially revised version of
another one. A re-working of the earlier series 'Night Sea
Crossing' (twenty performances in various locations, 1981–
87) as 'The Artist Is Present', the signature performance
at MoMA's show, involved Abramović sitting 'at a minimal
wooden table with two chairs awaiting museum visitors,
one at a time, who sit opposite her so that they can blankly

1

stare at each other for however long the visitor can endure' (Jae Emerling, 'Marina Abramović', 2010, p. 29). Would-be participants formed long lines each day, arriving well before MoMA was scheduled to open so as to have an opportunity to participate in the more than 730-hour performance (the sum of MoMA's opening times over the show's eleven-week run). For 'The Artist Is Present', members of the public could sit across from Abramović for as long as they chose: for some, this was a matter of minutes; for others, it was the entire day. For celebrity visitors (James Franco, Colm Tóibín, Sharon Stone, Matthew Barney, and Björk among them), museum staff usually and unpopularly provided immediate access; for the public, there was almost always a very long wait. Performance critic Alisa Solomon stood nine hours in the queue for a chance that never came, as the 'day's ninth sitter, clad in a severe black monk's cloak, took up the perch around 12:40 and stayed put until closing time, 5:30' ('The Artist's Present', 2010). But Solomon described her experience, and that of the hundreds of people with whom she waited, as collaborative and productive, perhaps, she mused, even constitutive of 'The Artist Is Present': 'by day's end, I thought that maybe it was in this periphery, on the sharp, invisible edge between spectating and partici-pating, that the work's most compelling meaning could be found'. In other words, conventions of engagement were re-imagined for the various participants in the event, dislocat-ing and distributing the effects of Abramović's performance to a much wider frame of meaning-making activity.

Introduction

Why theatre and museums? When, in 1991, Charles Marowitz made his case to 'free' Shakespeare, it was to wrest productions of the plays away from 'museum replicas in painfully reconstructed Globe Theatre conditions' (*Recycling Shakespeare*, p. 58), a sentiment that suggested theatre – or at least imaginative, exciting theatre – might be an antonym for what is found in a museum. Yet theatres and museums have increasingly become symbolic and actual neighbours, sharing the task of providing entertaining and educational experiences that draw people to a district, a city, a region, and even a nation. As components of the cultural landscape, theatres and museums alike play a role in creating and enacting place-based identity. No wonder, then, that so many cities in the world have turned to them in order to sell their brand both at home and abroad. Examples as geographically disparate as London's South Bank, Las Vegas's The Strip, and Abu Dhabi's Saadiyat Island illustrate what has already become a twenty-first-century consensus, that theatres and museums are crucial to a city's vitality and appeal.

Methodologically, too, theatre and museums share common ground. When Janet Marstine, in *New Museum Theory and Practice* (2006), describes the decisions that museum workers make 'about mission statement, architecture, financial matters, acquisitions, cataloguing, exhibition display, wall texts, educational programming, repatriation requests, community relations, conservation, web design, security and reproduction' (p. 2), she elaborates a collaborative process comprising these myriad activities, almost all of which have an analogue in theatrical production. Museums are, as Carol Duncan observed in 'The Art Museum As Ritual', 'complex totalities that include everything from the building to the selection and ordering of collections and the details of their installation and lighting' (1995, p. 10). In short, both theatre and museums require an infrastructure supported by a diverse range of technical and intellectual skills, acts of interpretation and mediation, and, eventually, an audience.

Barbara Kirschenblatt-Gimblett makes an even more explicit comparison: 'Exhibitions are fundamentally theatrical, for they are how museums perform the knowledge they create' (*Destination Culture*, 1998, p. 3). Traditionally, of course, museums arranged their collections in predictable, linear narratives, committed to organizational categories intended to be definitive. Theirs was a stage of authority. Nowadays, however, museums are invested in challenging those heretofore unexamined principles of organization, shifting from display to experience and inviting a more collaborative process with visitors. Contemporary exhibitions often constellate around questions rather than a seamlessly presented point of view, or choose to lay bare the history behind a particular collection or acquisition. Thus, institutions strive to develop more animated and less rigid modes of delivery. To this end, as Kirschenblatt-Gimblett proposes, today's museum is a 'theater, a memory palace, a stage for the enactment of other times and places, a space of transport, fantasy, dreams' (p. 139). Museums are now charged by stakeholders to increase access and deliver education in entertaining ways, so little wonder, then, that they adopt performance strategies that evoke different kinds and qualities of experience.

Demographic analyses of cultural activity show that people who go to the theatre, concerts, and movies are also museum visitors (John Falk and Lynn Dierking, *The Museum Experience*, 1997, p. 16), and the clustering of cultural venues in entertainment districts or neighbourhoods adds to the likelihood of shared visitor communities. In their discussion of 'Museums As Flagships of Urban Development' (2003), Chris Hamnett and Noam Shoval comment: 'In post-Fordist economies where cultural images and attributes are now a key element in inter-urban competition, prestige museums are increasingly a desirable commodity to be funded, sought, and competed for, rather than simply being seen as a drain on the budgets of hard-pressed city governments' (p. 233). Within that economic model, both theatres and museums have become increasingly attentive to market segmentation, looking to differentiate themselves from competitor institutions, often by way of self-promotion that emphasizes accessibility, creativity, and the spectator's experience.

Yet museums traffic mostly in material designated as representing the past, while theatrical performance takes place resolutely in the present, ephemeral, resistant to collection. I will look at how museums have dealt with the knotty problem of staging theatre's ephemerality as exhibition, but the intricately enmeshed relationships between theatre and museums that contextualize the history of performance art provide a rich starting place for thinking through commonalities and differences. Early twentieth-century artists who posed radical challenges to both realist theatre and representational art figure predominantly in the museum: what major collection of twentieth-century art would not hold works by artists of Dada, the Italian futurists, surrealism, or the avant garde? These same artists informed the development of performance art and theory, especially in the United States (from Allan Kaprow's 'Happenings' in the 1960s and the intermedial work of Fluxus through to a performance such as Abramović's 'The Artist Is Present' in 2010). One generic quality of performance art has been to move between drama and art, stage and museum, so that theatre and performance studies scholars and visual arts scholars have each claimed the practice for their own discipline. Kaprow, according to performance studies scholar Richard Schechner, 'wanted to demystify art, debunk the establishment that controlled museums, and make arts that could be performed by anyone' (*Performance Studies*, 2006, p. 166), objectives that have an unanticipated resonance with mission statements for theatre and museums at the beginning of this twenty-first century.

This book engages a recent history of museums that starts with mid-twentieth-century attempts to de-institutionalize cultural practices of display and ends with theatricalized experiences, often aggressively promoted for their popular appeal: according to Abigail Levine's review 'Marina Abramović's Time', more than 750,000 people visited MoMA to see Marina Abramović, and many more followed a real-time web feed. Theatre and museums both are coveted commodities in the marketplace and, as I hope to show here, are productive interlocutors in thinking about contemporary performance practices. In writing about the 'social turn' in contemporary art, Shannon Jackson asks whether new practices 'break institutional boundaries or set the scene for the recuperation of sociality by a service economy hungry for de-materialized encounters?' (*Social Works*, 2011, p. 44). This suggests at least some of the stakes in putting theatre and museums into the same conversation, and, in this context, I explore crossover critical issues that include paradigms of presentation and engagement, authenticity and re-presentation, and liveness and memory.

The subject of theatre *in* museums runs parallel to the interests of this book. Recent scholarship on this topic has addressed, both practically and critically, the use of live performance by museums to provide 'an "encounter" with a past that is "brought to life", peppered with "events" and advertised through a list of "What's On"' (Anthony Jackson and Jenny Kidd, *Performing Heritage*, 2011, p. 1). Whether through first-person interpretation or larger-scale re-enactment, this kind of theatrical activity functions as 'a challenging living history education method in which interpreters transform themselves into people of the past' (Stacy Roth, *Past into Present*, 1998, p. 3) and 'enhance the visitor's appreciation and critical understanding' of heritage (Anthony Jackson, 'Engaging the Audience', 2011, p. 23). Notwithstanding the proliferation of museum

7

theatre that this body of scholarly work explores, *Theatre & Museums* seeks a broader framework to examine strategies of 'narrativization and performativity' generally deployed in contemporary museum settings (Jens Andermann and Silke Arnold-de Simine, 'Memory, Community, and the New Museum', 2012, p. 4). Increasingly complex relationships between creative productions and their consuming publics require approaches that are deliberately inter-genre and inter-disciplinary, and this book looks at a variety of museum practices that speak to and with critical vocabularies in theatre and performance studies. At a historical moment when differentiation of 'theatre' and 'performance' is no longer the fraught territory it once was and when cultural institutions seldom hold firmly to a single category of creative output, silos of scholarly activity that most academics profess seem less and less suited to the conditions of contemporary cultural practices. *Theatre & Museums* is, then, a provocation that hopes, at the very least, to open up one track of such critical exchange.

From display to experience

The history of museums has been extensively researched and amply discussed. It is not my purpose here to replicate at any length the debates that predominate in that field. Rather, I sketch initial concepts for the public museum as background to a trajectory of general movements in museum practice from collection and display to pedagogy and participation. This modulation involves a turn to theatricality, driven by a new museology that thinks of exhibition 'as process rather than product' (Marjorie Halpin, 'Play It Again, Sam', 2007, p. 50). It is, I suggest, an emphasis on the texture of visitor engagement that drives the revisioned museum and aligns its practices so directly with contemporary performance.

What we recognize as the modern, public museum has its origins in the Enlightenment period and underwent rapid development throughout the nineteenth century. The Vatican's museums date from around 1750; the world's first national museum, the British Museum, was founded in 1753 and opened in 1759; and, under the authority of the French ministry of the interior, the Museum Central des Arts (later to become the Louvre) opened in 1793 to display paintings from the collections of the royal family and aristocrats who had absconded after the Revolution. Tony Bennett has provided a thorough account of this genesis in *The Birth of the Museum: History, Theory, Politics* (1995), in which, as the subtitle hints, his subject is scrutinized primarily through a Foucauldian historiography. Thus, for Bennett, the public museum emerged as a new modality of government power, since 'culture was increasingly thought of as a resource to be used in programmes which aimed at bringing about changes in acceptable norms and forms of behaviour and consolidating those norms as self-acting imperatives by inscribing them within broadly disseminated regimes of self-management' (p. 23). At a historical moment when revolution was palpably an option, strategies to better and more predictably control a nation's people were urgently sought and the museum was designed to foster an improved (which is to say, compliant) population. In theory, as Bennett suggests, it was intended that a museum setting would engineer 'a regulated commingling of classes such that the subordinate classes might learn, by imitation' (p. 28).

Before the advent of the public museum, collections (such as those in France) had been chiefly in private hands, accessible only to the very few of a city's or country's elite. The creation of what we now recognize as the modern museum came about in the transfer, willing or otherwise, of those private collections for public display. In the case of the national museum, a government typically constructed a building to house an already assembled collection that had been gifted by an exceptional (and exceptionally wealthy) individual – both parties moving ahead with an underlying belief in the capacity of the museum to act for the public good, although not always without financial benefit to the donor. For example, plans for the British Museum were initiated after the bequest in 1753 of physician Sir Hans Sloane's extraordinary private collection of more than 70,000 objects. Sloane wanted his collection to remain intact and, in this hope, bequeathed it in his will to King George II on behalf of the nation in return for a £20,000 payment to his estate. An Act of Parliament established the museum, and it opened in 1759 in Montagu House, a building on the same site on which the museum stands today (see <http://www.britishmuseum.org/the_museum/history_and_the_building/general_history.aspx>).

The three distinct departments into which the British Museum was initially organized suggest the importance of categorization to the emergent museum. These were

'Manuscripts, Medals, and Coins; Natural and Artificial Productions; and Printed Books, Maps, Globes, and Drawings. A fourth – Antiquities – was added in 1807 that contained such rarities as the Rosetta stone' (Edward P. Alexander and Mary Alexander, *Museums in Motion*, 2008, p. 59). Traditionally, museums have housed a collection of objects arranged in particular taxonomies that determined the fundamentals of display. The curator's task, once a collection had been acquired, was to research and provide a description for each object, to catalogue those findings, and to organize the objects in a display that was securely based on chronology and connection. Each item could be provided with a carefully annotated label and located in a group that would assert hierarchical relationships between the objects so arranged. As Nicholas Serota has observed about conventional gallery wall displays, how paintings are grouped 'places a curatorial *interpretation* on the works, establishing relationships that could not have existed in the minds of the makers of these objects' (*Experience or Interpretation*, 2000, p. 8; emphasis in original). In other words, any act of display is also always an act of mediation.

If the display of a collection was intended to produce an authoritative matrix of meaning, museum buildings (large, imposing, and generally in prime city locations) had an equally significant function in the creation of a public social sphere. Mieke Bal, in her 1992 essay 'Telling, Showing, Showing Off', describes this as the museum's literalization in the monumental that defines 'an era of scientific and colonial ambition' (p. 560). In this way, as museum culture developed during the nineteenth century and into the early part of the twentieth, remarkable energy and determination were demonstrated by prosperous industrial communities in propagating this power symbol of a place's economic and cultural presence, albeit often delimited by governmental agendas at local, regional, and national levels. Museums were 'typically located at the centre of cities where they stood as embodiments, both material and symbolic, of a power to "show and tell"' (Bennett, *The Birth of the Museum*, p. 87) – an arrangement that continues today, although, as I will suggest, with a somewhat modified legibility and purpose. Few of us forget the ubiquitous field trips to museums (and, indeed, theatres) from school days that emphasized the importance of particular kinds of cultural experience to the development and maturity of the educated person.

If the motivation behind museum inauguration had been so emphatically to educate and thus improve visitors, the extraordinarily robust economies in Western countries in the latter part of the nineteenth century (largely produced, of course, by colonialism and the industrial development it benefited) changed the focus of museum practice. Civic commitment was superseded by a private philanthropy that underwrote the rapid expansion of collections, most obviously in the museums of the United States, with the purpose of celebrating the newly affluent through a display of aesthetic and cultural sophistication. Harold Skramstad has noted extensive accumulation during this period of 'masterpieces of the artistic and cultural patrimony of Europe and the Orient, and these treasures began to find a permanent home in America's museums. As a result, museums began to focus less on the care of audiences and more on the care of their valuable and quickly expanding collections' ('An Agenda for Museums in the Twenty-First Century', 2004, p. 120). Thus, a professional museum practice evolved that was much more enthusiastically concerned with research, evaluation, and the creation of an archive than it was with its visitor population. Nonetheless, in an era when few people had the opportunity to venture far from home, much less go abroad, the museum collection, as Melanie Smith points out, 'traditionally served as a form of surrogate travel' (*Issues in Cultural Tourism Studies*, 2003, p. 87) – an education in the rest of the world delivered through a museum's acquired and categorized objects organized into narratives designed to affirm the superiority of Western cultures and the primitivism of everywhere else.

As energy and cash began to be directed most vigorously at acquisition, museums increasingly saw themselves, as Skramstad describes, as having a singular, and elevated, role as preservers and protectors 'of the rare, the unique, the beautiful, and the special in the arts, the humanities, and the sciences' ('An Agenda', p. 121). Even museums that more willingly retained a sense of duty 'to be a missionary force on behalf of popular education' (ibid.) did so in ways that equally affirmed the values of white Western masculinist culture as those by which everyone must be measured. For example, Tony Bennett, in *Pasts Beyond Memory: Evolution, Museums, Colonialism* (2004), describes the American Museum of Natural History (AMNH) 'as a bridgehead into the threatening sea of potentially unassimilable difference represented by New York's immigrant population' (p. 124). He argues that during the first decades of the twentieth century, this museum was urged to play a role in 'transforming the migrant child from an external threat into an active and willing prop of government' (ibid.). Perhaps for this reason, then, the AMNH was an early proponent of theatricalized displays in order to construct an all-absorbing narrative for the viewer, in this case putatively impressionable migrant children who, it was believed, would take what they learned back to their socially deprived home setting and neighbourhood in a kind of endless ripple effect of self-improvement. As Bennett trenchantly comments, 'The migrant child continued to occupy centre-stage in the AMNH's educational activities well into the twentieth century, albeit often more from the point of eugenic rather than political or cultural integration' (p. 125). Nonetheless, by the standards and principles employed by the vast majority of museums during this period, the AMNH's ongoing involvement with schools and its abiding commitment to teaching children about the collection were both radical and different.

The AMNH was an innovator in the design of displays. As early as 1913 it hired Carl Akeley, who had already achieved fame for his novel development of dioramas as mounting environments for mammals and other species (more information can be found at <http://www.amnh. org/museum/history/index2.html>). With origins in Louis Daguerre's diorama entertainments staged in public parks in the first half of the nineteenth century, Akeley's own dioramic experiments may well have been the beginnings of the theatrical turn in museum exhibition and an early technology that Bal suggests contributes to 'visual persuasiveness' ('Telling, Showing, Showing Off', p. 592). Dean MacCannell, in his ground-breaking book *The Tourist: A New Theory of the Leisure Class* (1976, 1999), describes this kind of display as a 're-presentation', a term to which I'll return in the next section of this book. He writes:

> A re-presentation is an arrangement of objects in a reconstruction of a total situation. Re-presentation always requires an arbitrary cutoff from what would have surrounded it in its original context, a frame, and usually a certain amount of filling in on the part of the museum: painted background, façades of native huts, department store mannequins for the period costumes. (1999, p. 78)

As MacCannell observes, although dioramic re-presentation is most often a feature of a natural history museum, it has also been exploited to create other kinds of scene. His example is Constantin Brâncuşi's studio on display in the basement of the Musée de l'Art Moderne in Paris, 'allegedly exactly as it was when he died, every tool in place' (p. 80). In the tradition of the Sloane bequest that became the core of the British Museum, Brâncuşi's studio – and even its mode of exhibition – was prescribed in the sculptor's will. In this case, then, the meaning of Brâncuşi's production as an artist is delivered in the micro-particulars of his studio rather than in a format that might educate or engage the viewer in some interrogation of artistic production, Modernism, sculpture, the decidedly mixed response to the artist's work in his own lifetime, or his canonical reputation thereafter. The production of authenticity (witnessed in the plenitude of detail) relies instead on the visitor's attentive scan – absorbing the uniqueness of the re-presentation of the artist's studio, a realist scene that is supposed to put the visitor in contemplative contact with the assumed genius of Brâncuşi. As Marstine has pointed out more generally,

> One of the longest-standing and most traditional ways to envision the museum is as a sacred space. This is an iconic image to which many museums still aspire. In the paradigm of the shrine, the museum has therapeutic potential. It is a place of sanctuary removed from the outside world. Museum collections are fetishized; the museum as shrine declares that its objects possess an aura that offers spiritual enlightenment as it inspires Platonic values of beauty and morality. (*New Museum Theory and Practice*, p. 9)

This idea of the museum as a shrine or sanctuary requires quiet and passive spectators to complete its purpose. Not surprisingly, then, it has been the idea most attacked in contemporary moves towards a more experiential museum practice, open to the participatory meaning creation of its visiting public.

Theodore Low's 'What Is A Museum?', published in 1942 by the American Association of Museums, is often referenced as a watershed intervention, addressing explicitly diminished interest in education and the commitment in its stead to acquisition directed at a type of knowledge production that was determinedly encyclopaedic, definitional, and expert. Low's essay spelled out the ideological divide between elite collection and popular exhibition, between preservation and access, and between institutional infrastructure and mandated activities. The question he had posed, Low contended, could not in fact be answered with any precision:

> When a specific museum is mentioned, the scholar thinks of the magnificent collections and perhaps of his favorite objects; the man on the street thinks of a huge pseudo-something-or-other building with pigeons flying above and peanuts on the sidewalk in front. One could find a definition for most museums if one started with a 'dynamic force in the cultural life of the community' and went down the list to 'a collection of buttons.' Most would be nearer the buttons, but in any case such a procedure does not help us. (p. 31)

Low's description here, I would argue, has been depressingly accurate far beyond the date of first publication of his seminal essay, and it is only over the past twenty years or so that museums have begun to produce the kind of answers that Low sought out.

Much more recent debates about the role of museums have still often repeated the string of oppositions that Low enumerated in his 1942 essay. Andrea Witcomb, for example, introduces her book *Re-imagining the Museum* (2003) with an account of an acrimonious dispute between the directors of the National Museum of Australia and the Museum of South Australia about the proper role of museums, played out in the pages of a national newspaper. Witcomb describes their exchange as reflective of 'the general tenor of many contemporary discussions on museums drawing on a familiar series of oppositions between traditionalists and renovators, objects and multimedia, objects and ideas, education and edutainment'. She continues: 'Depending on which set of values and practices a museum chooses it is then characterized as either elitist or popular, hierarchical or democratic, old and musty or new and exciting, irrelevant or relevant to contemporary concerns' (p. 2). If some measures of museum practice are new, the terms of their engagement are not.

But new museum theory, Marstine optimistically proposes, 'is about decolonizing ... it embraces many viewpoints' (*New Museum Theory and Practice*, p. 5). To overwrite the public museum's genesis and expansion during the peak years of European colonialism and American economic growth and power, new approaches to the exhibition challenge the production of a single coherent interpretation and instead provide many points of entry that the viewer might interrogate and weigh. Decolonizing, Marstine suggests, should inspire visitors to act as 'critical consumers' (p. 5). This is a practice that I will suggest in a later section relies on deeply performative effects. Visitors are no longer imagined in hushed contemplation but are given a much more active role. They are conceived as collaborators, at the very least, in the production of a museum's meanings. Falk and Dierking, in their aptly titled *The Museum Experience* (1997), were among the first to propose a visitor-centred model of thinking about the museum so as to elaborate 'the total experience, from the moment the thought occurs to someone to go to a museum, through the remembrance of the museum visit, days, weeks, and years later' (p. 1). This is an approach similar to my own in *Theatre Audiences* (1997), in which I emphasize the importance of a spectator's 'culturally constituted horizon of expectations' in selection, experience, and memory of the theatrical event (p. 211).

But, if the history of critiquing traditional museum practice, from Theodore Low to Tony Bennett, has concentrated on the institution's asymmetrical distribution of power – what Bal bluntly names 'comprehensive collecting as a form of domination' ('Telling, Showing, Showing Off', p. 560) – others have looked to open up more productive spaces to imagine this more active and engaged visitor. Witcomb, for example, takes Bennett to task for the limitations of a theory focused so single-mindedly on the political sphere. She comments: 'The effect of this is to obscure two other histories of the museum – a history of popular pleasure spaces and a history of economic interests in the museum' (*Re-imagining the Museum*, p. 17). I will return to the possibilities of pleasure in the experiential museum, but here it is important to acknowledge new museum theory's vested interest in economic paradigms that inform contemporary exhibition. Arguably, the most significant challenge to the old notion of museum-as-shrine has come in contemporary realities of museums and other cultural infrastructure as market-driven entities. Corporate sponsorship has, for the most part, superseded individual bequests in securing the economic health and viability of the museum, a fact that is especially vivid in the current financial dependence on the blockbuster – what Andrew McClellan has described as a 'steady diet of Impressionism, mummies, and anything with "gold" in the title' (cited in Marstine, *New Museum Theory and Practice*, p. 12). Nick Prior notes that these popular shows are not 'merely exhibitions, however, but also opportunities to sell large quantities of merchandise' and that 'the commercial spin-offs from these shows range across all commodity forms' ('Postmodern Restructurings', 2008, p. 515) – a practice that is familiar to the audiences of mega-musicals and other large-scale theatrical events such as Cirque du Soleil shows and rock concerts.

The dispersal of activity beyond the collection proper to ancillary activities ranging from lectures and workshops to the ubiquitous shops, cafes, bars, and restaurants has become commonplace in promotion of the contemporary museum. No longer, then, is the visitor implicated only as viewer of the display (with a hope on the part of the museum, at least sometimes, of transformative results); she is hailed as participant in a multivalent dynamic designed to animate the museum space, outside and within. The job of the visitor is to experience the environment on offer, and so, as Valerie Casey has concluded, 'museum installations give greater attention to the visitor's perceptual and aesthetic experiences in the context of other consumer experiences, rather than the former attention given to present an authoritative cultural narrative' ('Staging Meaning', 2005, p. 80). Ironically, much of the expansion of building space and activities is explained by museums as a re-commitment to education, a desire to bring more people through the doors to learn. This is not, of course, education as it was conceived by the founding fathers of national museums, but a legitimating endpoint for practices based on what Prior calls 'the "soft" values of consumption, distraction, and spectacle' ('Postmodern Restructurings', p. 509). Nonetheless, 'education' has proved to be a useful byword and has precipitated innovative strategies to encourage access and new commitments to diversify audiences, as well as to justify expanded obligations in the sphere of marketing.

The move to a vivified concept of education has produced a synergic turn to theatricality. Museums generate revenue through ticket sales or grants or both, and to attract sufficient admissions volume have increasingly sought out ways to incorporate visitors in active roles in the creation and experience of the exhibition. As Chris Bruce asserts, museums now follow 'a service economy ideal of putting the audience member at the center of the institution's mission; architectural environment, content, and presentation are inherently at the service the visitor's pleasure'

('Spectacle and Democracy', 2006, p. 131). More generally, new collaborative models in museum practice have come to resemble in very many ways the practices of theatre. It is both production and reception components that generate meaning and stimulate pleasure. In this context, like theatre, the museum is understood as the nexus of, among other things, the neighbourhood in which it is situated; architecture, galleries and other space; curatorial principles and methods; exhibit content and ancillary events; and spheres of reception (critical and public).

The case studies that follow look at these attributes as a range of performances directed towards the participatory visitor. Duncan would describe these examples as evidence of the museum as ritual, enacted by its audience: 'The museum's sequenced spaces and arrangements of objects, its lighting and architectural details constitute a dramatic field – a combination stage set and script – that both structures and invites a performance' ('The Art Museum As Ritual', p. 12). How the visitor engages such a theatricalized environment was precisely the subject of German photographer Thomas Struth's 'Museum Photographs' (Marian Goodman Gallery, New York, 1990). This work, a series of photographs of museum visitors looking at exhibits in landmark European and American museums, sets up nested frames that convert visitors into art and art into contextual setting. Do the spectators of Struth's photographs imagine themselves producing a 'live' version of what he records or do they recognize their own bodily presence as a re-performed consumer experience of which they are merely the most recent instantiation? Ruth HaCohen and Yaron Erzahi note that Struth's series provokes viewers to recognize that 'encounters between art and the public are expressions of liberal democratic norms aimed at preserving the authenticity of individual experience in the context of the larger group' ('Musing Spaces', 2010, p. 177). More importantly, they suggest that Struth's photographs demonstrate 'the representation of the public museum as a site for observing the ways in which art and the social order are coproduced in our time, how the meanings of experiencing art objects are adjusted to the norms and behavioral codes of the contemporary democratic order' (ibid.). In short, museums provide another site where contemporary performance takes place and, in this way, contribute to how we understand the production of theatricality as a deeply political and economically charged practice that reaches far beyond the confines of conventional theatre space. Struth's photographs remind us, too, that even the most immersive theatrical experiences – where we become participant-subjects in the drama – are produced, and constrained, by ideals of the social turn.

Re-performance

While Struth's photographs aestheticize the viewer's experience in a museum, Marina Abramović's oeuvre suggests a more animated challenge to how we interact with a collection. Her decision to include in the MoMA retrospective five earlier performances that would be re-presented by other actors directly interrogated the role of the museum in acts of preservation as well as the perennial question of performance art: is a work necessarily attached to the body of the artist who originates it? Of the five re-staged pieces, two had originally been conceived and performed as collaborations with Frank Uwe Laysiepen, Abramović's partner of some twelve years and better known as Ulay. Holland Cotter described the earlier Ulay–Abramović work in his *New York Times* review of the MoMA show:

> In one of these, 'Rest Energy,' they faced each other and together held a large bow and arrow. Ms. Abramović grasped the bow while Mr. Laysiepen pulled the string taut, aiming the arrow at her heart. . . .
>
> For the 1977 'Imponderabilia' they stood naked and unmoving inside the frame of a museum doorway, forcing people going from gallery to gallery to squeeze between them. In the same year they sat back to back, their long hair braided together, for 17 straight hours. Both pieces, and several others, have been recreated for the MoMA show, using performers trained by Ms. Abramović. ('Performance Art Preserved, in the Flesh', 2010)

Abramović's re-performances were predictably controversial: for some puzzling and for yet others shocking. Paul Ardenne described them as 'a radical solution to the apparent oxymoron of a museum exhibition of performance art, something that by definition is a unique event. Rather than simply revisiting the archives, this exhibition opted for reloading the event in the present moment through the acts of other people. What should we make of this?' ('Marina Abramović', 2010, p. 79). The artist had her own response to Ardenne's question, proposing re-performance as 'the best way to deal with the history of performance art and the accompanying demands of institutions. She contends that it is a way to take responsibility. . . . Abramović asserts that it is necessary for these works to be "reperformed" not to recreate or negate their initial historical, culture, or political context, but rather as a way to keep the gesture of the work vital for practicing artists, and not just for art institutions' (Jae Emerling, 'Marina Abramović', p. 29).

In this context, Abramović was surely able to act out an inevitable tension between the work itself and the work in the institution (here, MoMA). Among other things, her strategies laid bare a dependency on theatricality both to exhibit the condition of history and the archive and to satisfy 'liveness', a quality that Philip Auslander has explained as involving a 'simple logic that appeals to our nostalgia for what we assumed was the im-mediate: if the mediatized image can be recreated in a live setting, it must have been "real" to begin with' (*Liveness*, 1999, p. 38). Especially interesting, for this reason, is Levine's account of her experiences as one of the artists involved: 'As one of the 39 reperformers who took part in the exhibition, I confronted the issues brought up by the retrospective and reperformance from a perspective deeply embedded in the experience of Abramović's performance works. I spent more than 120 hours in near stillness in the galleries, as others made their way through the experience of the show' ('Marina Abramović's Time'). Levine's analysis of re-performance is revealing precisely because of its 'insider' status. I quote the following passage at length to prepare for some later discussion of theatricality, experience, and memory. Furthermore, the account points to an oscillation between ephemerality and preservation exploited in Abramović's MoMA show. Levine asks:

> How would these reperformances stand next to the mythology of Marina and Ulay's performances, as well as the material-documentary remains of the works? We struggled with these issues for their theoretical and historical interest, but more immediately in our commitment to create affecting experiences for our audience within the structures we were given. . . .
>
> Reperformance must, essentially, become performance, an exchange in the present. If the reperformances become effective only in relation to the 'original' performance of the work, then they become a fragmentary form, another document. The curation of the MoMA show moved the reperformances, to an extent, towards reception as documentation. Of course, the very nature of a retrospective, a look back at an artist's career, points to this historical, at times didactic, focus. Additionally, each performance was placed next to video documentation of Abramović

performing the work, as well as explanations of the original context and, at times, the changes made to the work.

The process described here by Levine is exemplary of museum practice invested in authority (the sheer ability to stage a retrospective of a major figure's work and to provide expert information about the documentation on display). This performance looks a lot like the act of 'filling in' that MacCannell described as 're-presentation' in the production of the AMNH's dioramas to show off their acquisitions. What is new, however, is Abramović's extension of the archival palimpsest, to give her audience the pleasures of immediacy and experience which documentary material, however dazzlingly displayed, simply cannot. It worked for MoMA and Abramović both to have visitors witness video documentation of an original 'Imponderabilia' only after squeezing past the naked actors in the doorway involved in its re-performance. This is all about making a spectacle in the 'live' moment and elaborates a remarkable faith in the signification of a three-dimensional body. But it may be, too, that the 'live' is less powerful in its effects than the 'authentic'; Christopher Grobe notes of his visit to the show that, 'with their backs turned to the performer, six people huddled around a small television screen watching footage of Abramović herself performing the 1997 "original"' ('Twice Real', 2011, p. 108).

In an examination of emotional responses stirred up by these re-performances, Jae Emerling attempts to think through the creative possibilities of repetition, noting that 'No one claims that a reperformance of Samuel Beckett's *Endgame*, for instance, is an attempt to recapture the "original thing," which never existed anyhow except as a script, as a potentiality. Each reperformance is a repetition; each repetition is not simply different, but it is *difference* as such' ('Marina Abramović', pp. 29–30). While Emerling's point in this last sentence suggests a productively Derridean destabilization of ideas of authenticity and originality, even as it forgets the rigid authority Beckett and his estate for a long time exercised over the staging of his plays, for the purposes of interaction between theatre and museums, it also raises the question of what happens to theatre when it becomes the subject of exhibition. Can an artistic medium defined by a commitment to liveness continue to perform as a record of its own past? Diana Taylor, in her deservedly influential book *The Archive and the Repertoire: Performing Cultural Memory in the Americas* (2003), contrasts 'the *archive* of supposedly enduring materials (i.e. texts, documents, buildings, bones) and the so-called ephemeral *repertoire* of embodied practice/ knowledge (i.e. spoken language, dance, sports, ritual)' (p. 19; emphasis in original).

Her argument rests on the archive's power to separate evidence, the source of knowledge, from the knower, while the repertoire 'enacts embodied memory: performances, gestures, orality, movement, dance, singing – in short, all those acts usually thought of as ephemeral, nonreproducible knowledge' (p. 20). Abramović's commitment to re-performance, then, is one way of asserting active repertoire

in the context of apparently static archive. Her re-performances consider the value (commodification) of her body as
the 'authentic' subject collected for the institutional archive
even as that same body is rendered absent in the varieties of
documentation that record the earlier work. By commission-
ing other bodies to re-perform the same work, Abramović
makes a compelling case for decoupling performer from
performance – a coupling that, in performance art, has long
been held as a guarantor of authenticity. Other case studies
that follow look at instances where repertoire intrudes upon
narratives constructed by museum-as-archive (the collection) and how these performative acts provide new ways of
engaging history, identity, and everyday life.

Theatre in the museum: collection as performance

Conversations, academic and otherwise, commonly cite the
fact of liveness (Auslander's cautions notwithstanding) and
the condition of ephemerality as distinguishing the unique
and special qualities of theatre. To be part of an audience is
to enjoy a direct, 'of the moment' relationship with what-
ever is being performed. Theatre takes place in the present
and museums create from the past. But neither the friction
of this contradictory relationship with time nor the trust
invested in what happens 'live' is as straightforward as
we sometimes imagine, a fact ably articulated in Levine's
description of the Abramović re-performances. Certainly,
for theatre scholars and practitioners, there is often a
compelling desire or need to access performances after

the fact. Evidence, such as it is, usually comes from print materials (published and unpublished scripts, programmes, prompt books, etc.), reviews, and, in more recent years, video recordings of the live event. Less often, costumes, set designs, props, and other material remains can be consulted. At best, each of these elements is little more than a clue about what a performance might have been like, how a production brought together all its constituent parts so as to entertain (or bore), and they may, in the end, offer no more than memory – a condition that inspires Dennis Kennedy to describe performance as 'a kind of museum': 'To be precise it is not the performance which has literal museum characteristics but rather the desire to remember it ... which leads to cataloguing, critical memory and the tendency to decorporialize the event' (*The Spectator and the Spectacle*, 2009, p. 197).

Some theatre companies and a few libraries devote significant resources to the collection and maintenance of these befores-and-afters of the thing itself, but it has been rare for them to find their way to larger public audiences. Occasionally artefacts from earlier productions of a play might be displayed as a contextual aspect to a new production of the same play, photographs and other ephemera from an actor's career might accompany a performance in which he or she appears, and so on. This is the stuff of theatre lobby displays. These scenarios are composed to inform a singular perspective, that of the audience, and to enhance their encounter with the live performance. But it is altogether a different challenge when theatre in general becomes the subject of a museum's display.

The history behind the development of a national theatre museum in the UK is a long and troubled one, even if its origins were, not surprisingly, in the form of a gift from a theatre maven and collector. In 1924 the Victoria and Albert Museum (V&A) – the national museum for the decorative arts – accepted Gabrielle Enthoven's 'vast collection of playbills, programmes and cuttings, which she continued to fund and update until her death in 1950' (Margaret Benton, 'Capturing Performance at London's Theatre Museum', 1997, p. 26). After the acquisition in the 1970s of other theatre-oriented collections and, at last, some government funding, the Theatre Museum was established as a department of the V&A. In 1987, the museum opened in Covent Garden, a prime location in London's theatre district, although the subterranean space was small, chilly, and remarkably unsuited for the task at hand. With very little opportunity to display any large part of the collection, the London Theatre Museum was primarily a working archive, generally busy with people consulting files or reviewing videos of productions the museum had recorded (a resource to which I'll return).

Margaret Benton has offered useful insight into the difficulties inherent in establishing the Theatre Museum's curatorial principles and practice. She writes:

> Live performance exists only in the present, a momentary and unrepeatable communication

between performer and spectator. Are performing arts museums then not a contradiction in
terms, an attempt to preserve the unpreservable,
to record the unrecordable? Certainly the shards
of performance that make up our collections . . .
can only ever provide a very partial record of
the live event. Other museums have to grapple
with the problem of documenting and interpret-
ing the ephemeral, but the material vestiges of
events rooted in common life-experiences have
the nostalgic appeal of 'how we used to live' – of
past Utopias. Theatre aims to transport people
out of the ordinary and into a journey of imagi-
nation. Edmund Kean's sword, his death mask
or an engraving may fascinate an enthusiast of
nineteenth-century British drama, but how can
such relics convey the magnetic presence of an
actor who once held London audiences in thrall?
('Capturing Performance', pp. 25–26)

They simply can't. And the Theatre Museum's use of traditional strategies of display (a choice determined at least as
much by its tiny budget and limited space as by more philosophical concerns) certainly failed to reproduce the appeal
of Kean on the stage or, indeed, of any live performance.
The problem for a museum of theatre and performance is
not the lack of an archive, but precisely its possession of it.

Benton also notes that the Theatre Museum could not
compete with 'the popular, interactive displays to be found

in most new museums' (p. 26), ironically more theatrical than one taking theatre as its subject. A review in the 1990s led to a pragmatic downscaling of activities and, for the first time, clearly articulated acquisition policy. It also resulted in what the museum saw as its boldest stroke: the creation of the National Video Archive of Stage Performance. This strategy, Benton reports, aimed to 'provide the best, most detailed and currently available method of documenting what would otherwise disappear altogether' (p. 27). The parameters for recordings destined for the Video Archive, as Benton describes them, are worth further examination:

> An archival recording differs in intention, and usually in practice, from cinema and television coverage of live performance, the main aim of the latter being to produce public entertainment. The purpose of an archival recording is to convey as faithful and as detailed a record as possible of the original stage performance for the practical use of the theatre industry, vocational training, academic research, schools and colleges. It should aim to be an eyewitness to the event taking place in the presence of a live audience, ideally from the point of view of a single spectator in the theatre, and should cover all the action. Cameras should be as unobtrusive as possible. There should be no change to the original lighting or setting, nor should the audience be disturbed in any way. (pp. 27–28)

Commitment to educational purposes is paramount, but not to the education of a general public. Rather, the target audience for this documentation is either the interested specialist or the student. The description also suggests that minimizing technological intervention will allow the recording to come closest to capturing liveness (actors and audience) and, therefore, to convey verisimilitude. As Taylor reminds us, however, '[a] video of a performance is not a performance, though it often comes to replace the performance as a *thing* in itself (the video is part of the archive; what it represents is part of the repertoire)' (*The Archive and the Repertoire*, p. 20; emphasis in original).

Of course, much more recently, audiences have had regular opportunities to see so-called live film versions of performance through the extensive distribution to cinemas of shows by high-status producers such as the Metropolitan Opera in New York and the Royal National Theatre in London. Remarkably, in the first National Theatre production I saw on screen (Alan Bennett's *The Habit of Art*, 2010), the cameras were left running in the intermission, making the South Bank spectators an odd, and apparently oblivious, mirror to the cinema audience as well as the object of its scrutiny, something that gave the filmic experience an unexpected illusion of liveness. Other productions I have since seen cut away from the theatre auditorium during breaks to show previously recorded interview and other 'bonus' features more typical to a film on DVD. In these and many other ways, the mediatized 'live' has become both more familiar and less denigrated. Yet, following the museum display of Abramovic''s performances and Taylor's definition of repertoire, it is clear that performance is not at all the same thing when it fails to have a body. This is a dilemma, inevitably, for a museum concerned with building its performance collection inside an objective of preservation. As Robert C. Morgan argues, the absent original body is not something easily resolved by re-performance: 'to contemplate the exigencies of performing a work of body art by an artist from another time ... based on extant documentation, archived to the teeth, is like transferring a four-by-five-inch photographic negative into a digital image' ('Thoughts on Re-performance, Experience and Archivism', 2010, p. 1).

Ongoing financial struggles shut the Theatre Museum in 2007, only twenty years after it was established and even in the face of concerted protests from members of the broad theatre community. Dominic Cavendish, writing in the *Daily Telegraph* ('Don't Bring Down the Curtain', 2006), called the closure an act of 'wanton cultural vandalism'. But the V&A did not neglect its theatre collection for long, and in March 2009 new Theatre and Performance galleries opened in renovated space in the main South Kensington building. If the old London Theatre Museum had inadvertently fallen into the traps of the traditional museum (too much emphasis on serving a connoisseur community under the guise of education, and too dull and restricted in its presentational strategies), then the design of these new galleries sought to correct those shortcomings through more spectacular display and the incorporation of interactive experiences that were, by then, commonplace in a museum setting. These new galleries hold objects from across the spectrum of performing arts. Theatre and popular music predominate, but there are at least samplings of other forms, including dance, opera, pantomime, circus, and music hall. Better yet, the galleries assiduously avoid old taxonomies of display and instead opt for thematic constellations that take visitors through various renditions of creativity. Grouped under gerundial titles of 'Creating', 'Staging', and 'Experiencing' performance, items of interest are shown without overdetermining reference to genre or chronology; instead they are clustered to represent a particular phase of activity. 'Creating', to take one example, houses digitized pages from play manuscripts along with information about financing, casting, and venues (brief descriptions of the gallery rooms are available online: <http://www.vam.ac.uk/page/t/theatre-and-performance-galleries/>). Cumulatively, the aim is to provide visitors with a comprehensive sense of production (a behind-the-scenes tour in many ways) alongside an archive of performance effects.

While a breadth of historical periods and genres is represented in the various exhibits, emphasis is firmly on the more recent. The intention, I suspect, is to foster a spirit of entertainment through visitors connecting with aspects familiar from performances they may have seen live or recorded. The galleries are also punctuated with hands-on elements – costumes to try on, stage effects to create, and others. Many film and sound illustrations of performances are incorporated, drawing on the museum's own video archive and adding materials that allow directors, designers, actors, and others to explain their process, so that the viewer gets apparently expert information. First reviewers of the new galleries almost all delighted in a reproduction of Kylie Minogue's dressing room replete with scattered shoes – a populist re-performance of the Brâncuşi studio – and in the remarkable range of stage outfits and memorabilia belonging to some of the world's most famous and most theatrical pop stars, Mick Jagger and Elton John among them.

The blending of high and low culture, and the careful selection of what Benton usefully called 'the shards of performance' ('Capturing Performance', p. 25), give the Theatre and Performance galleries a lively and engaging feel – actively illustrating a 'something for everyone' approach. The exhibit relies on pleasure in recognition, where the display of some trace of performance is always synecdochic, a stand-in for the past event. In this sense, the galleries summon their visitors to convert archival memory into repertoire through their own affective responses, triggering re-performance in the spectator of what once was experienced live if not by them, then by others. For my own part, there was a moment of delight in the recognition of Brian Eno's iconic 'feather collar' costume. But what, I wondered, was it supposed to mean, and what work was it supposed to do as 'performance'? What were visitors to learn from its belated display? That it was worn by Eno on the very first Roxy Music tour (1972) might be a prompt for personal or generational nostalgia, but what does that actually tell us about the costume? Or Brian Eno? Or the band? Is it enough that it serves as an aide memoire for something experienced long ago? Or the wish it had been seen long ago? Or is it simply a three-dimensional artefact familiar largely from its frequent photographic reproduction? It's still a very theatrical stage costume, but in 1972 it was unusually so. Moreover, in the national museum for the decorative arts, it would have been provocative to explore the costume's backstory, that it was made by Eno's girlfriend at the time, accomplished ceramicist Carol McNicoll. Could this one remnant open up the history of the 1970s British music scene, or consider the impacts of visual culture (and especially pop art) in the conceptual performances that Roxy Music developed? Both figuratively and literally, then, the costume lacked content. No interrogation, or even old-fashioned interpretation, of its cultural moment and, of course, no Brian Eno. It was, in the end, a performance of absence. So it is hard to disagree with Sarah Frater's review of the Theatre and Performance galleries ('Capturing the Art of Performance', 2009): 'The contrast between the vitality of the stage and the inert theatrical afterlife haunts the V&A's big scale galleries that cover live performance in Britain over the last 350 years.... [D]espite the obvious curatorial care, you wonder if this museum of live performance isn't an oxymoron.' Or, put another way, perhaps it is an archive of things that have been permanently lost. On the one hand, then, this might seem to produce the melancholic viewer, offered nothing more than a Proustian taste of what once was; on the other, it may well be more valuable – trusting to the same viewer for the active production of memory and meaning.

Similar problems of display prevail at Shakespeare's Globe Exhibition, advertised as 'the world's largest exhibition devoted to Shakespeare and the London in which he lived and worked'. The exhibition, in a space adjoining the replica Globe Theatre on London's South Bank, involves more sound and video archive (including documentation of workshops and productions at the theatre), a costume collection, and various interactive displays intended to give visitors an experiential connection to the theatre of the early seventeenth century. There are research components (impressively, the work done on clothes of the period – what people wore on and off stage, what materials they had access to, the patterns and cutting techniques used), but most, like the objects in the Theatre and Performance galleries, are designed to provide a behind-the-scenes look at production. There are a number of opportunities to operate stage effects that experts conjecture were used on the Elizabethan stage, demonstrations of sword fighting, and touch-screens providing information about the city in Shakespeare's time. Very much the V&A's early modern correlative, Globe Education also seems like another poor and rather dull relation to live performance, in this case made all the more so by the knowledge that the 'real thing' happens on the Globe's stage, just footsteps away.

Occasional museum exhibitions about theatre fare little better. 'Drama and Desire: Artists and the Theatre', an exhibition at the Art Gallery of Ontario (AGO) in Toronto from 19 June to 26 September 2010, was intended to be that year's summer blockbuster and opened to a positive reception in the *Globe & Mail*. James Adams, in a review titled 'The Gallery As Theatre, the Artist As Drama Queen', enthused:

> What's new is the sheer theatricality of the display. Drama & Desire isn't so much presented as staged, its mother-lode of dramatic paintings, by masters such as Jacques-Louis David, Dante Gabriel Rossetti and Henri de Toulouse-Lautrec, supplemented and surrounded by props, models, special effects and live performances. It's all very, well ... *playful*, an acting-out of the ways that gesture and pose, décor and lighting, incident and character onstage have informed imagery on canvas, and vice versa. (2010, p. R5; emphasis in original)

The idea was provocative: to put theatre and painting into dialogue across history (for this was an exhibition firmly anchored to artistic movements and narrative chronology travelling from the French Revolution to the First World War). If the backbone of the show was a history of visual representation of the stage, remnants of actual performances complementing the visual arts record in each room offered the visitor more theatrical takes on both period and movement. Props and costumes from the vaults of Ontario's Stratford Festival and others from the Canadian Opera Company and Toronto Public Library archives added a three-dimensionality to an otherwise conventional, if beautifully lit, gallery wall display. Adams notes: 'For fans of interactivity, there are wind and rain machines to hand-crank alongside *The Storm, Antigonus Pursued by the Bear*, Joseph Wright's epic 1790 recreation in oil of a scene from Shakespeare's *The Winter's Tale*' (p. R5). The AGO boasted that its wind and rain machines were authentically eighteenth century, but the V&A and the Globe exhibition have them too, and perhaps the repetition in all three venues of just these effects best illustrates how few theatrical things to do museums have, as yet, conceived.

'Drama and Desire' did offer live performance in the galleries on weekends: on Saturdays, four actors from the Canadian Stage TD Dream in High Park production of *Romeo and Juliet* performed and, on Sundays, the city's Opera Atelier presented *Degas and His Dancers*. Daily, the exhibit was animated by actors in costume; on my visit, the facilitator was a young man in a floor-length blue velvet cloak with large ruffled cuffs and collar, an outfit that put me immediately in mind of the museum replica performances of Shakespeare that Marowitz so hated. The actor's task was to perform a character and declamatory style suited to the gallery in which he was to be found, a job he took on with enthusiasm and with some radical museum theory of his own as he confessed to always moving through the rooms in reverse chronological order 'just because that's not the way you're supposed to go'. But summer blockbuster the exhibition was not, ending up, in the words of *Toronto Star* entertainment critic Martin Knelman, more of a 'Drama and Debacle' ('AGO Loses $3M on Costly Flop', 2010).

The show lost $3 million and attracted a miserly 54,209 visitors (34,000 were AGO members, for whom admission was free). Notably, the exhibition that had closed to make way for this theatre-based show, 'King Tut: The Golden King and the Great Pharaohs', had garnered a visitor toll exceeding 400,000 (ibid.). Of course, it had both mummies and gold in the title – guaranteed, as McClellan promised, to pull in the crowds (cited in Marstine, *New Museum Theory and Practice*, p. 12). Theatre and art, or at least the AGO high-end versions of these forms, appealed to hardly anyone.

It is tempting to end this section with nothing more than Chris Wilkinson's summary of the fate of theatre in a museum setting. Writing in *Guardian Unlimited* ('Noises Off: Museums Can't Capture the Essence of Theatre', 2009), he asks: 'Is there any point in exhibitions about theatre? I have to admit that when the Theatre Museum in Covent Garden closed down, I couldn't bring myself to care very much. At its core, theatre is live and transient – two things that are by their nature impossible to exhibit in the static and conservative confines of a museum.' But if the V&A's Theatre and Performance galleries, Globe Education, and 'Drama and Desire' give much truth to Wilkinson's charge of impossibility, Experience Music Project (EMP) in Seattle – Chris Bruce's exemplary 'post-museum' – suggests, rather differently, a commitment to performance. For EMP, the live and the transient animate the collection and require active visitor engagement in the production of history.

The experiential museum

Experience Music Project's roots are much like many other museums': a wealthy benefactor with a collection that needed a home. Microsoft executive Paul Allen had built up an extensive collection of materials from and about the life of one of Seattle's most famous sons, Jimi Hendrix, and he assembled a team to think about how best to put this collection into the public domain. Of course, museums which start from the ground up – new building, new mandate, new curatorial policy, not to mention a whole lot of money – have a decided advantage in innovation over their older counterparts that must work within and around a substantial history of collecting and exhibiting in their established architectural space. Allen's team took its inspiration from a contemporary success story, the new Guggenheim Museum (1997) as engine of regeneration for the Spanish city of Bilbao. They commissioned Guggenheim 'starchitect' Frank Gehry to design for Allen's Hendrix-based ambitions: 'A classical music fan, Gehry wanted to understand rock 'n' roll so he traded in his Bach for Hendrix and took a trip to the neighborhood guitar store. Gehry bought several electric guitars, took them back to his office and cut them into pieces. The guitar pieces were the building blocks for an early model design. Influenced by the colors in the early model, Gehry's final design brightly displays the red and blue hues of electric guitars' (<http://www.empmuseum.org/aboutEMP/index.asp?categoryID=157>). The street-level look, like that of its Bilbao predecessor and Gehry's later Disney Concert Hall in Los Angeles (2004), is disruptive; it is a building that flaunts its difference from its milieu and performs deliberately as a postmodern pastiche of what a museum is supposed to look like: 'The building sends the initial message of the institution as destination, and acts as a very specific tool in connecting with and even *determining* an audience type that possesses a high curiosity quotient and sense of adventure. The building announces that you're going someplace different, someplace a little weird but also exciting' (Bruce, 'Spectacle and Democracy', p. 137; emphasis in original). In other words, Gehry's EMP, even from the outside, is a highly theatricalized place, its opening in 2000 an arresting addition to the otherwise rather tired Seattle Center, previously best recognized for its once futuristic icon of the 1962 World's Fair, the Space Needle.

EMP's interior is equally unconventional: non-linear and multileveled, its spatial arrangement visibly rejects an old-style organizational logic typical of museums in favour of dramatic, occasionally dizzying, impact: 'Like a Las Vegas casino, EMP does not hold back once you get inside. In fact, once inside, you tend to forget the outside. Density of content complements the intensity of the architecture. The effect is to obliterate the everyday world. You have entered a spectacle and you are in its grasp' (Bruce, 'Spectacle and Democracy', p. 138). In short, from first sight, EMP is designed to be experienced, a live and improvisational performance of its own terms, and to walk through the doors is to enter the action on its many stages. While Bruce is right that EMP is a content-dense locale, it scarcely appears that way to the visitor, because space, format, and methods of engagement mask exhibit in favour of activity.

Specifically, Bruce considers that 'EMP pushes the envelope of the museum-as-attraction' (p. 131), praising the willingness of the design team to draw not just on the best of new museum practices within a mandate to educate, but also from the 'entertainment strategies of a theme park' (p. 132). He concludes: 'It is a model of what a museum might look like when it gets every populist, technological and interactive wish it ever dreamt of – a spectacle of architecture and multimedia displays that attract, inform, and seduce its visitors' (ibid.). This attempt to do things differently, as well as the emphasis on a populist context, is inscribed in EMP's mission statement:

> EMP is a leading-edge, non-profit museum, dedicated to the ideas and risk-taking that fuel contemporary popular culture. With its roots in rock and roll, EMP serves as a gateway museum, reaching multigenerational audiences through our collections, exhibitions and educational programs, using interactive technologies to engage and empower our visitors. At EMP, artists, audiences and ideas converge, bringing understanding, interpretation and scholarship to the popular culture of our time. (<http://www.empmuseum. org/aboutEMP/index.asp?categoryID=285>)

'Risk-taking' and 'empowerment' are not words generally associated with museum mandates (no doubt Theodore Low would be shocked). But EMP is deliberate in its self-promotion as an anti-institutional institution – fitting, for sure, to the business of rock and roll. According to Bruce, 'EMP assumes that active involvement *empowers* the visitor to have the confidence to perhaps uncover untapped wells of creativity and self-expression. At heart, EMP asks the question, "If a poor black kid from Seattle (Hendrix) can change the world as we knew it, why not you?"' ('Spectacle and Democracy', p. 135; emphasis in original). Meaning and experience are in the hands, literally, of visitors, suggesting that EMP is as much a repository of performance tools as a rock and roll archive. Originally Allen and his team avoided including the word 'museum' in the name, preferring 'experience' to suggest active engagement and, obviously, to acknowledge its inspiration and top-billed star, Jimi Hendrix. The museum assumes that if visitors are to learn about the history of the American popular music that EMP so avidly collects, then they need to perform as part of it.

Interactive spaces include 'On Stage' (as the EMP guide describes it, 'You, a guitar and a virtual stadium of screaming fans. Purchase a DVD or poster to immortalize your performance') and 'Sound Lab' ('No matter your age or skill level, see how it feels to play electric guitar, drums, keyboards and other instruments'): collection as repertoire in the hands of the visitor-performer. Certainly the museum mobilizes much of the same nostalgia for the live event that the V&A Theatre and Performance galleries summon in their own presentation of rock star memorabilia, but at EMP, while visitors may well have an identical response in admiring a guitar once played by Hendrix, the iconic silver glove worn by Michael Jackson, or the turntables used by Grandmaster Flash, they also get to lay down a track that puts them into the story through embodied experience. This extends what might otherwise be an inspiration and affirmation of memory into an affective practice of re-performance.

Well-planned technological infrastructure and careful policies ensure everyone gets his or her turn in the recording booth without too long a wait, and, once in the booth, there is a large menu of songs that can be accessed and 'learned'. Even the inexpert musician can do enough to accompany artists such as Hendrix, Led Zeppelin, or Alanis Morissette in a favourite song. Allen's deep pockets – Bruce calls EMP 'a \$250 million "gift" ... to the city of Seattle and the rock 'n' roll universe' ('Spectacle and Democracy', p. 146) – enabled EMP's designers to include as much technology as they could find a use for, but what works best, in the end, is not all that high-end infrastructure (although it certainly helps), but a crafting of the collection that inspires and endorses creativity in its visitors.

If visitor experience at EMP is built around participatory/live components, there are other, much more conventional museum functions that underpin these more obviously theatricalized aspects and reveal a more predictable relationship to museum planning. First, EMP has kept a focus on the region's music history. One of the more orthodox galleries, Northwest Passage, covers artists with origins in the area (Bing Crosby, Kurt Cobain, Heart, Pearl Jam, Soundgarden, among others), and recent feature exhibitions have followed this focus: 'Jimi Hendrix: An Evolution of Sound' (2008–10) looked at the artist's unique guitar sound and its continuing influence, and 'Nirvana: Taking Punk to the Masses' (2010–13) celebrates the Seattle 'grunge' scene. A well-designed website encourages engagement with the collection beyond the in-person visit; to coincide with the Nirvana exhibit, EMP's site asks its visitors to send in their own memorabilia and has an online gallery of 'user-submitted' Nirvana materials. Further, the archive of EMP's prestigious annual Pop Conference is available for free download from iTunes U, as are curriculum guides for its holdings, another option that extends the participatory frame from the physical to the virtual.

EMP's curatorial policy allows for nimble responses when things don't work: one of EMP's explicitly theme-park-styled attractions, a simulator ride, proved unreliable mechanically and thus costly (Bruce, 'Spectacle and Democracy', p. 149), so it was closed in 2003 and replaced with a Science Fiction Museum and Hall of Fame. This was obviously a cheaper option to maintain, attracted a largely different demographic, and, at the same time, enhanced EMP's stock in representing elements of American popular culture that have been mostly neglected by major museums elsewhere. The Science Fiction Museum (although not the Hall of Fame) was closed in 2011 in favour of feature exhibitions – such as James Cameron's 'Avatar: The Exhibition', another behind-the-scenes endeavour – that could respond more nimbly still to its target audience. Strategic re-performance of content is also evident in its latest branding tactic: 'EMP Museum: music + sci-fi + pop culture' (<http://www.empmuseum.org>), at last taking on the designation of 'museum' for its mash-up of experience-based content.

Casey suggests that, generally, experience-oriented visitors require more curatorial intervention as 'the processes of display used to convey information are often privileged over the particularity of objects' ('Staging Meaning', p. 84), and this is acutely realized in EMP's operational model, which inscribes collaboration, on site and off, as the core of its practices. With few permanent displays and content given shape through interactivity, EMP comes close to delivering on the live and transient experience of theatre that Wilkinson thought impossible in a museum setting. This requires, among other things, a commitment to ongoing novelty in its attractions and the confidence to let visitors literally make the show. Strangers engaging in impromptu jam sessions, friends who once went together to see Hendrix live reuniting, a devotee playing his way through the Bob Marley songbook – these people move through the museum on an invisible edge between spectating and participating (as Solomon said of the Abramović exhibition) or performing, an edge at EMP that emphasizes both knowledge and, avowedly, pleasure.

I hesitate to move from EMP, and its unabashed impulse towards edutainment, to my next examples, which are altogether more serious endeavours. But they, too, are experiential museums, and their strategies of engagement also require visitors who participate, through both scripted actions and performances of space. Let me turn here, then, to the Jewish Museum in Berlin, the Museum of Tolerance in Los Angeles, and the United States Holocaust Memorial Museum in Washington DC – museums that have the daunting task of explicitly displaying absence and inspiring ethical memory.

Daniel Libeskind's building for the Jewish Museum has been a destination since the moment of its completion; as Julia Noordegraaf writes, 'This building was so spectacular that it drew thousands of visitors before the collection had even been installed' (*Strategies of Display*, 2004, p. 209). In 1989 Libeskind had won an International Building Association juried competition, from 165 submissions, to design an extension to the existing Berlin City Museum to house a new Jewish Museum. Only a few months after Libeskind's commission, the Berlin Wall fell, and in the aftermath of this momentous event, plans changed and it was decided to repurpose the existing building (at one time the city's High Court) and to have both old and new serve as the city's Jewish Museum. The original building functions as the museum entrance, with classical gallery space for temporary exhibitions on its upper level; Libeskind's new edifice houses the permanent exhibition. Noordegraaf notes of Libeskind's architecture: 'The building has such an expressive force that for years the staff had problems setting up the exhibitions' (p. 209).

Like EMP, the Jewish Museum recomposed its contextual neighbourhood scene and animates the streetscape with a dense iconography. The older building, known as the Collegienhaus, is Baroque in style. Originally built in 1735, it was more or less destroyed during the Second World War, with only parts of the outer walls standing by the war's end. Rebuilt in the 1960s to house a newly established Berlin Museum, the Collegienhaus is little more than stage set, a re-performance of itself before the war (before the city's devastation and divide). The new building, replete with architectural drama, stands alongside the old: the two are not joined at street level, the only connection between them a passage below ground. Of the project, Libeskind has said: 'The task of building a Jewish Building in Berlin demands more than a mere functional response to the program. Such a task in all its ethical depth requires the incorporation of the void of Berlin back into itself, in order to disclose how the past continues to affect the present and to reveal how a hopeful horizon can be opened through the aporias of time' (cited in Bernhard Schneider, *Daniel Libeskind, Jewish Museum Berlin*, 2005, p. 19). In juxtaposition to the symmetry of the Collegienhaus façade, Libeskind's architecture performs a kind of disharmony. Its sheer concrete surface, slashed by so many seemingly random zig-zagged punctures, was conceived 'in part from imaginary lines of the city map which connect the site with the street addresses of great figures in Berlin Jewish cultural history – Heinrich von Kleist, Heinrich Heine, Mies van der Rohe, Rahel Varnhagen, Walter Benjamin, Arnold Schönberg' (p. 36). Thus, the museum's appeal to experience starts outside, seeking visitors and passers-by alike who might engage this encoded meaning. Klaus van den Berg interprets the exterior as 'a coexisting silent space, or invisible space, to restore the vanished Jewish community' ('Staging a Vanished Community', 2009, p. 232).

Inside, the experience constructed through Libeskind's building only intensifies. Leaving the Collegienhaus through a long hallway leading away from its basement, visitors arrive in the new space and must choose between two inclined pathways: one leads towards the Garden of Exile; the other to the Holocaust Tower. These routes are named the Axis of the Exile and the Axis of the Holocaust, symbolic representations of the fate of German Jews. Libeskind asserts they are 'two lines of thinking. . . . One is a straight line, but broken into many fragments, the other is a tortuous line, but continuing indefinitely' (cited in *Discovering the Jewish Museum Berlin*, 2005, p. 4). The Axes are punctured by six Voids, only some of which are accessible. The overall effect is disorienting, demanding, threatening even, with the space strikingly unfurnished by a museum's usual density of display and direction. Indeed, one area is always left empty and marked as such, to remind us of the art that we have lost, what those who died in the Holocaust might have made in longer, and freer, lives. Another area, known as the Memory Void, holds an installation by Israeli artist Menashe Kadishman called *Shalekhet* ('fallen leaves'). Here more than 10,000 mask-like faces cut from steel are piled on the floor – a memorial but also, the artist has suggested, an expression of hope for new life in spring (*Discovering the Jewish Museum Berlin*, p. 38). Visitors are invited to walk across the installation, their action (and especially the soundscape this produces) creating a dynamic performance. *Shalekhet*, then, conjures repertoire in the experience of archive.

There are glass display cases embedded in the concrete walls of both Axes, running almost all their length but without much height, connecting with the visitor at eye level. These contain objects, possessions (letters, suitcases, photos, clothes, baby toys, books, a teacup), and are donations from survivors for the most part, as the museum guide describes it, 'expressing their wish that a parent, cousin or friend be remembered in the country where they lived and felt they belonged, before being driven into exile or murdered' (*Discovering the Jewish Museum Berlin*, p. 7). But it is the affective pull of the building's architecture that most compellingly shapes visitor engagement. The Axis of Exile has a steep incline, representing the difficult journey of emigration, and ends in the Garden, a strange set of forty-nine large, inclined concrete columns filled with earth so that willow oak grows out of the top and forms a tangled forest atop the pillars. Libeskind calls this an 'upside down' garden: forty-eight of the columns are filled with the earth of Berlin to represent the formation of the State of Israel in 1948; the 'one central column', he says, 'contains the earth of Jerusalem and stands for Berlin itself' (cited in Schneider, *Daniel Libeskind*, p. 40). The other Axis takes visitors to the Holocaust Tower – a tall, bare, and unheated concrete space where a narrow slit close to the very top allows in only the thinnest glimmer of light. Visitors are asked to enter, alone or in small groups, and the heavy door is closed; it is a moment of grim surrogation. This experiential engagement has become the signature of Libeskind's museum design, although all components of this museum look to visitors to turn space into narrative.

The United States Holocaust Memorial Museum in Washington DC and the Simon Wiesenthal Center's Museum of Tolerance in Los Angeles also seek to create visitor experience by choreographing the audience's traversal of museum space. This is what Casey describes as 'architectural script'; she suggests of the Washington museum that the 'controlled path – colloquially known as the "funnel" – through the exhibits from the fourth floor to the first enables visitors to follow a well-defined chronology' ('Staging Meaning', p. 84). Similarly, the Museum of Tolerance dispatches visitors directly to the Holocaust Exhibition, a seventy-minute sound-and-light guided display arranged in a variety of rooms, with progress from one to the next controlled by the narrative. Electronic doors between rooms open only when commentary is completed; more like traditional theatre than a conventional museum, then, this exhibit insists on keeping its audience passively in place while the specifics of the scene unfold. Both American locations are dedicated to activating and sustaining social memory, and critics have commented that they have the unusual task of representing history that took place in geographies other than their own (although both point to the effects of American foreign policy and the circulation of anti-Semitic propaganda such as Henry Ford's writings on 'The International Jew: The World's Problem'), and they must make those events resonate with their predominantly American visitors. In *Spectacular Suffering* (1999), Vivian Patraka has persuasively argued that this is a performative process, with the potential 'to offer thousands of people the opportunity to change from spectator/bystander to witness' (p. 11).

To involve the visitor in active witnessing, both museums activate protocols of identification. Upon entry to the Holocaust Memorial Museum, the visitor is asked to become actor, presented with a six-page identification card. The cover states 'For the dead *and* the living we must bear witness' (emphasis in original), and other pages provide the biography of an individual who died in the Holocaust and whose story becomes an organizing script for the visitor experience. At the Museum of Tolerance, each visitor carries a 'passport photo card' with the story of a child whose life was changed by the actions of a Nazi-occupied Europe. In other words, visitors are charged to act as proxy for the absent other, enacting the core of the memorial component of these museums, or what Patraka movingly calls the condition of 'goneness'. She suggests this term as it 'reflects the definitiveness, the starkness, and the magnitude of this particular genocide by dictating the scope of what and who has been violently lost, including succeeding generations that cannot be' (p. 4), a description that speaks, too, to the empty room in the Berlin Jewish Museum's exhibition space.

At the Holocaust Memorial Museum my ID card gave me the biography of Juliana Nemeth, born in Hungary to a Jewish merchant family, married with three adult children, and running a hardware/grocery store in the small town of Szentes. Its middle two pages contain first-person entries, one for 1933–39 that briefly describes how the Nemeth family coped in the Depression years and another for 1940–44 that records four months of occupation by German troops, the confiscation of their store and home, and the forcible relocation of her husband and children to a 'makeshift ghetto'. Turning the page to my card's final entry, I learn that 'Juliana and her family were deported, via the Strasshof labour camp, to a labour camp in the east Austrian village of Goestling an der Ybbs. They were shot by retreating SS soldiers, just days before U.S. forces reached the area.' Most visitors scrutinize their ID cards while riding in the large steel elevator that runs to the fourth floor, where the Holocaust narrative begins – this is the first of many journeys in tight quarters with strangers, and the card provides a useful diversion. It functions to personalize the museum's project and to shape an act of witnessing by way of laminating a specific identity to each visitor through merging one particular story from the subject of display with the individual visitor experience. At the Museum of Tolerance, I held the passport of Jean-Claude, born in Oran, Algeria, in 1938, but whose family had moved to France just before the outbreak of war. Jean-Claude's mother was arrested and deported to Auschwitz (she survived), and his baby sister was hidden and cared for by French farmers, but Jean-Claude and his two older brothers were held at a children's home before they were sent to the gas chambers at Auschwitz in May 1944. Bold type at the end of the document tells me that 'Jean-Claude was one of 1.5 million Jewish children murdered by the Germans and their collaborators during the Holocaust'. The distribution of these reproduced documents inspires in the visitor what Alison Landsberg has termed *Prosthetic Memory* (2004, p. 2).

Casey has articulated the Holocaust Memorial Museum's reliance on 'staging techniques' to realize the Holocaust history, noting the 'visual and olfactory stimuli' that contribute to the visitor's grasp of 'the magnitude of the Holocaust horror' ('Staging Meaning', p. 84). Both she and Patraka pay particular attention to a room filled with shoes, a compelling signifier of missing bodies: 'despite constantly blowing fans, the shoes smell (from their own disintegration) and thus involve our bodies in making memory. The smell of the shoes is organic, like a live body, and in that way they become performers, standing in for the live bodies that are absent' (Patraka, *Spectacular Suffering*, p. 128). Tracy Davis asserts that the 'odor invades visitors' bodies and in so doing cements concept to experience' ('Performing and the Real Thing in the Postmodern Museum', 1995, pp. 35–36). This is perhaps the most powerfully somatic in a series of theatrical scenes in which visitors are gathered in unusually cramped conditions to act out, even if only in associative ways, the upheavals of quotidian life during the war. Patraka notes how the curved archways of the museum's main hall echo those of a train station, where the deportation process started (p. 123); later, visitors walk through a train car – a scenario, like many of the spatial configurations in the museum, which emphasizes overcrowded and unsettling conditions. Often visitors must strain to read relevant information or stand in close proximity with others to be able to hear a witness report. In contrast, the Holocaust Exhibition at the Museum of Tolerance eschews strategies that might suggest associative experience in favour of controlling visitors' engagement with the lesson at hand. Each 'scene' in the exhibit is mediated by three representational figures, made of plaster and scaled at approximately three-quarter size. They are introduced as the researcher, the historian, and the designer and while they are an inanimate presence in each of the rooms, the voice-overs that provide visitors with both information and interpretation are apparently theirs. As Patraka has noted, they function as characters in a play, with the spectator's task resembling that of the theatre audience: to listen in and to understand (p. 126). Outside the exhibition, the museum hosts the telling of stories by actual Holocaust survivors, offering several sessions each day, programming that re-animates the importance of 'liveness' in service of didactic objectives.

If the Holocaust story forms the core of the Museum of Tolerance, other exhibits there (both permanent and temporary) take on the broader field implied in the museum's name. As the museum stages it, there are two doors – one marked 'Prejudiced' and the other 'Unprejudiced' – with the visitor facing the apparent choice of which to pass through. Except that the 'Unprejudiced' portal is firmly locked, performatively parsing an assessment of the contemporary world. The museum's Tolerancenter addresses injustices of recent and contemporary history: human rights violations, genocide in Bosnia and Rwanda, and hate speech among them. The last of these forms the subject of

'The Point of View Diner', a re-performance of a 1950s diner, fully chrome and red vinyl, with a menu of controversial topics on video jukeboxes and large, wall-mounted screens that would elsewhere be tuned to a sports channel. A filmed case study precedes audience response on each topic: we watch a scenario and offer our opinions through a voting mechanism that tabulates answers from across the diner. Nostalgia for an *American Graffiti* idealism of 1950s America is melded with *Who Wants to Be a Millionaire?* game show interactivity. The 'trivia' we display here is attitudinal, intended to evaluate our (lack of) tolerance.

These experiential museums are committed to social engagement, often grounded in the specific context of public memory, and, particularly in the cases of the Holocaust exhibits, a directed pedagogy. They recognize what Paul Connerton has described as a purposeful structuring of memory: 'we all come to know each other by asking for accounts, by giving accounts, by believing or disbelieving stories about each other's pasts and identities. In successfully identifying and understanding what someone else is doing we set a particular event or episode or way of believing in the context of a number of narrative histories' (*How Societies Remember*, 1989, p. 21). To convey and sustain memory, he argues, we need performance, and so these museums construct participatory experiences to produce their distinctive versions of the past and require visitors to give them life. Anna Reading reminds us, however, that 'activity . . . is not the same as agency' ('Digital Interactivity in Public Memory Institutions', 2003, p. 73). Is it also the case that these experiential museums merely keep us busy, impelling us, quite literally, to complete their script? Johannes Birringer has perhaps captured it best: 'Participation is a strange current fetish' ('Dancing in the Museum', 2011, p. 48). Contemporary cultural consumers want/need to be part of the action, but outcomes can be coerced as much as inspired and their pedagogical impacts hard to measure.

Performance as collection: repertoire in the museum

What I have charted so far is a direction in museum practice that runs from display to experience, from tableaux to performance, and from quiet contemplation of authoritative interpretation to active participation that implies the collaborative production of meaning(s). This shift has required the introduction of practices that explicitly draw on repertoire to supplement the archive, as well as expanded interpretive horizons. The experiential museum challenges the idea that collections comprise the orderly arrangement of things past and promotes instead a performative present that might make history anew. The 'strain between ... the archive and the repertoire', as Taylor identifies it, involves difference in transmission, storage, and dissemination (*The Archive and the Repertoire*, p. 24). She notes: 'It is only because Western culture is wedded to the word, whether written or spoken, that language claims such epistemic and explanatory power' (ibid.). My final three examples, museums devoted to the lives of North American native peoples, look at interpretive strategies that attempt to exhibit cultural practices that do not rely on the word or the archive, but reside only in repertoire – to cite Taylor again, traditions 'stored in the body, through various mnemonic methods, and transmitted "live" in the here and now' (ibid.). These are sites that challenge the idea of the museum and expose Western cultural assumptions that pertain even in the more experiential instances that I've described so far.

The National Museum of the American Indian (NMAI) is the sixteenth of the Smithsonian Institution's museums in Washington DC, and its primary site opened on the Mall in 2004. Its holdings (more than 800,000 objects) are founded on a collection built up by George Gustav Heye which was previously displayed in part in his private museum in New York City. As the NMAI's advertising puts it, 'We are the place where America's history begins.' Another museum building with a spectacular exterior presence, the NMAI's curvilinear form imitates the wind-carved rocks characteristic of America's southwest, and its evocation of the natural is enhanced by detailed contextual landscaping – a meadow of native plants, crops grown using native agricultural methods, and forty 'grandfather rocks', so called as 'they are the elders of the landscape, welcome visitors to the museum grounds and serve as reminders of the longevity of native peoples' relationships to the environment' (James Volkert et al., *National Museum of the American Indian*, 2004, p. 23). The building and surroundings together inscribe difference from other sites on the Mall, itself an exemplary location of mainstream institutional culture. Moreover, the NMAI's act of differentiation extends beyond the Mall to the larger context of America's capital city, where government is everywhere, a powerful reminder of its dismal and often cruel history of 'managing' indigenous peoples.

The NMAI incorporates a rich iconography, much of its composition obscure if not illegible to the non-native eye. The architectural design team included contributions by the highly regarded Douglas Cardinal (Blackfoot, architect of the Canadian Museum of Civilization), as well as Johnpaul Jones (Cherokee/Choctaw), Donna House (Navajo/Oneida), and Ramona Sakiestewa (Hopi) (Volkert et al., *National Museum of the American Indian*, p. 27), in pursuit of its goal to tell a story 'of Indian cultures as living phenomena throughout the hemisphere' (p. 26). Interior space addresses native cosmology, the American Indian experience from the perspective of eight specific groups, story telling, and traditional knowledge – attempts to represent, interpret, and celebrate cultural practices that are fundamentally oral and performed. Interactive display and hands-on engagement are appropriately, if predictably, deployed with a view to educating a non-native visitor.

Tellingly, first reviews of the museum were neither generous nor enthusiastic. Edward Rothstein, writing in the *New York Times* ('Museum with an American Indian Voice', 2004, p. E1), accuses the museum's inclusive curatorial strategy of 'monotony' and its displays of appearing as 'homogenized pap', as if 'every tribe is equal, and so is every idea. No unified intelligence has been applied. Moreover, with a net cast so wide, including South and Central America as well as Alaska, the only commonality may be the encounter with colonizers.' If Rothstein seems here to refuse to engage the NMAI on its own terms, his brutish assessment points to the tensions inherent in this museum, its subject, and its addressees. Kevin Coffee, in an essay on 'Museums and the Agency of Ideology' (2006), takes Rothstein to task as he asserts that 'empowerment is not about permission; it's about self-determination. How the story of native peoples is to be told is precisely a matter of "whose voice" – and the fact that so many came together to enable the exhibitions of NMAI may likely reflect how well the museum's mission resonates among those very stakeholders' (p. 444). For the usual (read, non-native) museumgoer, it is one more collection to be consumed – with luck, critically. For native populations, this is long-awaited recognition.

Not accidentally, a threshold exhibit at the NMAI concerns the indigenous peoples of local Chesapeake, Algonquian tribes that were decimated during the first century of English colonial presence. The NMAI has as its first order of business the creation of a place that recognizes site-specific history at the same time as it promotes a longer and more inclusive 'American' history. This is not, then, the texture of visitor creativity that the playful design of the EMP inspires or the more sombre performances of Holocaust memorialization; rather, it is a resistant act. This is perhaps why Rothstein so easily misses the point, as the NMAI stands outside curatorial logic as it has developed in the West. Instead, the NMAI produces performative space appropriate to knowledges of the people whose stories it tells. In one of its galleries I witnessed an exchange between a native man and a non-native visiting with his young family. The native man was angry at the speed with which the children were moving through the gallery space, their interest in little but the opportunity to push buttons or touch-screens. He explained to their father that this was an act of disrespect, to which the father offered the apologetic defence that these were just little children. This moment illustrated the challenges of a 'contact zone' (to borrow Mary Louise Pratt's useful term from her 1992 book *Imperial Eyes*) that encompasses the museum's two intended audiences: its mandate promises, on the one hand, to 'advance knowledge and understanding of the Native cultures of the Western Hemisphere' and, on the other, 'to support the continuance of culture, traditional values, and transitions in contemporary Native life' (<http://americanindian.si.edu/subpage.cfm?subpage=about>). As an experiential museum, it raises the question (*pace* Coffee above), Whose experience matters?

The Heard Museum in Phoenix, Arizona, is also devoted to indigenous culture, and its genesis followed the familiar pattern: a significant collection had been assembled by Dwight and Maie Heard, and the museum opened in 1929, shortly after Dwight's death, with Maie acting 'as museum director, curator, custodian, lecturer and guide' (<http://www.heard.org/about/history.html>) until her death in 1951. Since that time, it has been run as a private, non-profit museum, with most of its $10.6 million annual budget funded by admissions. The museum houses extensive holdings of native art and artefacts, but my focus here is an interactive display that mobilizes performance as a vital tool in engaging both native and non-native visitors to think through embodied experiences of memory.

'Remembering Our Indian School Days: The Boarding School Experience', a continuing exhibition at the Heard, offers a multivalent and moving account of the US government's seizing native children from their homes and sending them to boarding schools, sometimes hundreds of miles away and for several years at a time. This is a policy that ran from the late nineteenth century well into the twentieth, although this history is rarely well known by non-native communities. Indeed, many do not know it at all, but its legacies remain deeply felt by native peoples. As Karl Hoerig explains in 'Remembering Our Indian School Days' (2002), 'The Indian boarding schools were created with the intention of assimilating Indian children into Euro-American culture by removing them from their home environment and immersing them in a closely controlled, Christian, English-only environment' (p. 642). The reality was impoverished living conditions, limited and poor-quality food, cruel disciplinary practices, and the determined obliteration of native languages. The founder of the Carlisle Indian School, quoted in Hoerig's account, understood that his responsibility towards each pupil was to '[k]ill the Indian in him and save the man' (ibid.).

At first encounter 'Remembering Our Indian School Days' appears to follow traditional curatorial principles: the displays look like updated versions of Akeley's dioramas designed to fill in and interpret material objects that remain as traces of the boarding school experience. The first of these, a powerful symbol of the transition from native community to residential school, is a barber's chair:

> Accompanied by incessant sounds of clipping and snipping scissors and surrounded by long dark locks of hair littering the floor of the exhibit case, the chair stands as the final threshold between home life and indigenous culture and the industrialized, Anglicized world of the boarding school. As is evidenced by former students' memories and by the infamous and ubiquitous 'before and after' propaganda photos of Indian children, changing the students' appearance was the first step in usurping control of their bodies and minds and 'killing the Indian.' (Hoerig, 'Remembering Our Indian School Days', p. 643)

As Hoerig suggests here, the barber's chair is re-staged through a variety of interpretive sources: re-performances of its use (the intense soundtrack of clipping noises), photographic evidence of its outcomes, and accounts from former students about its psychological impacts. Yet, while visitors move through rooms sequentially, the displays and these other interpretive features do not always synchronize. Testimonies from native 'informants' interrupt a visitor's relationship with the material display and intervene in what might otherwise be a singular temptation to see the native student as victim. Certainly, the ugly realities of life in one of these schools are palpable by way of the arrangement of objects and provision of print text interpretation: there is ample evidence of the punishments meted out for speaking in native tongues, the prevalence of infectious diseases, and the numbers of children who died at these schools. But the testimonial interventions exceed a narrative of suffering and deprivation. The many voices describe friendships with other students and occasionally with a teacher, the things they enjoyed (often sports), major and minor acts of rebellion, and other times of shared pleasure. The exhibit shapes an ambiguous interpretive space and marshals affect towards a more grounded knowledge of the social, material, and economic effects that this government policy produced.

Participatory elements in the exhibition further complicate the range of response. If one track of interpretation follows conventional curatorial display and another emerges from first-hand description (delivered via sound and video installations), a third turns to creative practice. Various tasks require the visitor – if only in passing, and safely – to embody the native child's experience of a school. There are elementary punishments to fulfil (those copying-out exercises of 'I will not ...' that were given to all disobedient schoolchildren for much of the twentieth century and are familiar still from the opening credits of *The Simpsons*) but also some more difficult assignments. Hoerig explains: 'Given a blue book, the visitor is invited to "Select your new name. Write your name on your booklet. Put any additional information on the first page of your booklet." From the six options for boys, I chose Benjamin Record. According to the brief personal history I was given, I was now five hundred miles from home, and it would be five years before I saw my family again' ('Remembering Our Indian School Days', p. 645). Much like the ID card at the Holocaust Memorial Museum or the profile handed out at the Museum of Tolerance, this is an exercise in prosthetic memory likely to provoke an emotional response. At the Heard, however, the visitor is not the passive recipient of a new identity but must literally perform it in the act of writing – prodding authors to imagine bearing these new names as their own from this moment of inscription. Boarding school administrators knew that the eradication of native names short-circuited transmission of knowledge about a family's relationship to the land and to each other, and that the assignment of a prescriptive identity, affirmed in writing, would subjugate that body to Western governance. This was an act that brought the outlaw body into the scope of the archive – a repressive action in which every non-native visitor is implicated. But 'Remembering Our Indian School Days' also incorporates elements that directly address its native visitors, asking them to record memories of boarding school – their own or those of family members. This invitation re-asserts repertoire against archive and reminds non-native visitors that their acting out of identity is but a temporary substitution for another's lived experience.

My final example is Blackfoot Historical Crossing Park (BHCP), museum of the Siksika Nation, developed to promote and preserve its people's language, culture, and traditions

(<http://www.blackfootcrossing.ca/aboutus.html#name>).
Situated some sixty miles east of Calgary, Alberta, on Siksika
(Blackfoot) land, BHCP is located at the site of the signing
in 1877 of Treaty 7 between First Nations people in what is
now southern Alberta and the colonial British government.
The treaty outlined a claim on the land for the Crown and
laid out conditions for compensation, as well as allocation
and use of the land, for the indigenous groups. This document still forms part of Canadian law. BHCP does not use
the word 'museum' in its self-description but names itself
simply as 'place'. Its mandate promotes a performance-oriented, culturally specific range of activities:

> The central concept of the Blackfoot Crossing
> Historical Park is that of a Meeting Place.
> Storytelling and oral tradition will be used to
> communicate the culture of the Northern Plains
> Indian to Siksika members and visitors. Cultural
> continuity will be achieved through tangible and
> intangible cultural examples of the Siksika way
> of life: tribal art, costumes, archaeological sites,
> music, dancing and language. The prairie chicken
> dance, teepee circles, buffalo hide shirts, and red
> stone pipes for smoking tobacco, with unique
> red stripes for women and black stripes for men,
> are elements of the Blackfoot culture that are
> not found among other Plains Indian groups.
> (<http://www.siksikanation.com/blackfoot-
> crossing.html>)

Like the NMAI in Washington DC, the central building at BHCP (opened in 2007) is constructed to respect and incorporate native iconography. The website explains that every decision worked towards making a structure that represented icons sacred to the Siksika Nation (<http://www.blackfootcrossing.ca/architecture.html#design>). In addition to its prolific citation of teepee design, the front entrance is shaped to resemble the feathers of an eagle, the sacred bird of Blackfoot religious festivals; wall sconces inside the building represent the war or medicine shields used at pow-wows; the library is painted in colours that represent jingle dress dancing, a traditional performance component. Furthermore, the architecture is sensitively attuned to the contextual landscape: barely visible from the road, it does not obscure a panoramic view of the Blackfoot river valley, emphasizing the importance of the natural world in native cultures. Unlike the Experience Music Project, the Jewish Museum, or the NMAI, this is not a museum that intends to rescript its setting; every bit as dramatic as any of these other buildings, it looks instead to honour the surrounding landscape and acknowledge the stories of ancestors already in that place. In this way, BHCP participates in the repertoire of the land, a function that, to borrow from Taylor, 'keeps and transforms choreographies of meaning' (*The Archive and the Repertoire*, p. 20).

Inside the BHCP building, Treaty 7 is reproduced in full, with interpretive materials illustrating its far-reaching impacts on indigenous culture in the region, alongside a variety of other displays ranging from the medicinal use of native plants, through Canada's own history of residential schools, to celebrations of First Nations culture at the annual Calgary Stampede. On the land surrounding the centre, there are teepee camps (some available for overnight stays), interpretive walks, and an archaeological site where a dig is in progress to uncover a mid-eighteenth-century (thus pre-colonial) settlement. The Siksika Nation describe BHCP as their people's opportunity to present their story and thus expand Canada's history by 10,000 years. The experience of BHCP exceeds both building and contents since they cannot contain a people whose relationship to land is so fundamental; the visitor must move outside and literally walk the site to begin to experience the long history of place. This is, in a different context, Mike Pearson's point in *Site-Specific Performance* (2010): 'Walking then is a spatial acting out, a kind of narrative, and the paths and places direct the choreography. This regular moving from one point to another is a kind of mapping, a reiteration of narrative understanding. Different paths enact different stories of action for which landscape acts as a mnemonic' (p. 95). At BHCP, landscape is repertoire alongside the building's archive, and the visitor's interaction (walking) is not an act of keeping busy, but a deliberately meditative experience of place history.

All the other case studies in this book are based on museums in urban settings, and it is true that the vast majority of museums (and theatres) are city-based. BHCP is remote, on land that Treaty 7 allows the Siksika Nation to occupy; it is tangibly a destination that non-native visitors travel to. But it is also home and a gathering place for many First

Nations peoples. Each June BHCP hosts the World Chicken Dance Championships, an event that celebrates the pow-wow dances that originated with the Blackfoot people and that are now transmitted through competitive categories for juniors, teens, adults, and seniors. BHCP is, then, an active site for the preservation and incubation of its own performance culture. Similarly, the Heard Museum hosts each February the World Championship for Hoop Dancers, which it advertises as bringing the top seventy hoop dancers from across Canada and the US to compete. These events are museum practices as dependent on liveness as any theatre, and illustrative of Taylor's embodied acts that transmit 'communal memories, histories, and values from one group/generation to the next. Embodied and performed acts generate, record, and transmit knowledge' (*The Archive and the Repertoire*, p. 21).

'Recognizing performance as a valid focus of analysis', Taylor argues, 'contributes to our understanding of embodied practice as an episteme and a praxis, a way of knowing as well as a way of storing and transmitting cultural knowledge and identity' (p. 278). These exemplary museums of native culture each reveal the possibilities and potentials of a performance-oriented museum, and encourage performance scholarship to more assiduously address indigenous cultural practices. Particularly in the case of BHCP, the museum is construed as a living space, actively populated by and for the people it represents, and all three examples assert cultural performances that have been neglected in mainstream museological and other representation in ways that mark, to borrow from Coffee, a 'sharp arena of conten-tion' ('Museums and the Agency of Ideology', p. 445). From this perspective, the NMAI, the Heard, and BHCP suggest the limits of the modern museum and affirm the emergence of more experiential and inclusive exhibition practices.

Conclusion: re-performance matters

This book started by asserting the timeliness of more cross-over cultural analyses, with theatre and museums as one such matrix of investigation, traversed here with examples from Marina Abramović at MoMA to the World Chicken Dance Championships in southern Alberta. The selection is not dictated by any attempt to categorize 'good' museums or to emphasize progressive curatorial practices. Rather, the examples are chosen to illustrate strategies of exhibi-tion that rely on theatricality in different forms. In part this range of examples illustrates Casey's assertion that 'live performance in the contemporary museum has not only dispensed of the primacy of the object, but it has *become* the object' ('Staging Meaning', p. 85; emphasis in original).

In the study of theatre, we generally accept that there is an original (often thought of as authoritative) performance and that subsequent productions provide new interpreta-tions of an initial script. The Shakespeare industry provides the obvious example and relies on a shared belief, apparently able to transcend both time and place, that the re-perform-ance of his plays is worthwhile. This assumption has been much more fraught and contested in other spheres, including avant-garde performance and installation work. The MoMA

Marina Abramović retrospective crystallized many of the issues around re-performance, although she has certainly not been the only artist to explore this topic. Tino Sehgal has re-performed Bruce Nauman's 'Wall-Floor Positions' (1968) and Dan Graham's 'Roll' (1970) as *Instead of allowing some thing to rise up to your face dancing bruce and dan and other things* (2000, various locations, including the Stedelijk Museum in Amsterdam in 2005, the Walker Art Center in Minneapolis in 2007, and the New Museum in New York in 2008), and the Rude Mechanicals, an Austin, Texas, performance group, has developed its Contemporary Classics Series, which remounts 'happenings' of the 1960s and 1970s as closely to the original as possible (studying archival video and other documentation) so as to make accessible 'germinal works' for new audiences (<http://www.rudemechs.com/shows/history/beaver.htm>). All these examples affirm a trend towards reproduction of what was once thought of as material that could not be replicated and that, even if it could, should be restricted to its originator(s). And we might add to this spectrum of re-performance conditions an increasing reliance in theatre and performance studies on video documentation – the ubiquitous turn to YouTube for evidence to illustrate a performance practice in class or in a conference presentation. Not only is contemporary performance mediatized, so is the scholarly dissemination of both practice and theory in the field. This requires an examination of this category of re-performance from the full range of perspectives and motivations, since all these approaches affect what we value as performance as well as how we conceive of its history. In this context, Rebecca Schneider observes that Abramović 'sees the move into venerated art museums as ensuring her ability to control history from beyond the grave' (*Performance Remains*, 2011, p. 4).

Any discussion of history inevitably involves reference to the archive, and this is perhaps the most direct point of connection with museums and their necessarily more explicit engagement in this area. Theatre and performance studies scholars have wrestled with ideas of the archive theoretically, ideologically, and practically, with Diana Taylor's inflection of the repertoire a much-needed intervention in the challenges of effectively historicizing performance. Here I have taken up, from very different geographical settings and often to distinctively different ends, Taylor's project across archive and repertoire to look specifically at how museums treat the subject area of theatre and performance, as well as other performance-oriented cultural effects.

Of course, it is scarcely surprising that interrogations of archive emerge in the context of the museum: preservation and exhibition remain at the heart of the institution's mission. On the other hand, the archive, for theatre and performance historians, is very often less visible. Even the most traditional forms of theatre present problems for the researcher – what is legitimate evidence for scholarly inquiry: text? memory? performance shard? video document? Moreover, we might see reviews and criticism alike as, in many ways, their own re-performances of their subject. The stir around the Abramović retrospective suggests not just an interest (even a belief) in the value of 'liveness' to historiographic method but a preference, too, for the authentic (original) body.

Relationships between archive and repertoire in museum settings provide useful examples for thinking about the preservation of performance work as well as its revival in other possible settings and timeframes. Citing the Abramović show at MoMA, Tim Griffin (then editor of *Artforum International*) raised the problematic of 'performance and its historicization' in an interview with Dutch architect and urban designer Rem Koolhaas, who suggested, 'Maybe reenactment can exist only in a context-free environment. It would be unbelievably exciting if you could actually perform *Imponderabilia* in a shopping mall' ('Many Happy Returns', 2010, p. 287). While a context-free environment is surely impossible, the point here is important: how do different institutional contexts frame an original performance and at the same time limit the ways in which it might be re-performed, whether in the same place or elsewhere, at a proximate or remote historical moment, and therefore how it might be understood?

Further, the coupling of theatre and museums also provides for an expanded notion of the audience, congruent with contemporary preferences for what Jacques Rancière termed 'the emancipated spectator'. Elements of museum design inspire and demand activity, as van den Berg writes of Libeskind's Jewish Museum, a building transformed 'into a performance site challenging the visitor to participate in a cultural performance' ('Staging a Vanished Community', p. 238). Changes in expectations for museum visitors align with more participatory performances in many other formats, ranging from site-specific installations to flash mobs to competitive reality television programmes whose contestants' success or failure relies on audience votes. New kinds of cultural competency and behaviour are not only commonplace, but expected. Examples in this book suggest that strategies devised to include the visitor in the creation of experience invariably do so with pedagogical intent and sometimes as the primary means of producing multiple sites of interpretation, ambiguity over authority. Martin Hall takes a much less optimistic view of these newly animated forms of spectatorship, arguing that 'museums in the experience economy start not with institutions but with the individual, offering to those who can afford to participate the fantasy of a customized world, the opportunity to be who they want to be through the technologies of simulation' ('The Reappearance of the Authentic', 2006, p. 81). In other words, creativity in reception is one more consumable directed not at any social benefit but towards the instantiation and affirmation of an individual, premised on the economic wherewithal to participate.

Whether emancipated from or encumbered by the economics of late capitalism, visitor experience needs to be calibrated across a range of contexts and beyond rigidly separate disciplinary accounts. Moreover, it is surely time to think about theatre and museums together since so many others do: cultural policymakers, urban and regional planners, arts and other marketing agencies, and, of course, visitors. Crossovers between different cultural practices, institutional settings, and audiences suggest that scholarly inquiry must match this breadth of interest if it is to address the very many ways performance appears, engages, and disappears in this contemporary moment.

Further reading

Readers interested in gaining wider knowledge of the contemporary debates in museum studies should turn first to the useful and comprehensive anthologies edited by Gail Anderson (*Reinventing the Museum*, 2004) and Janet Marstine (*New Museum Theory and Practice*, 2006). Landmark texts underpinning the changes in thinking about the practices behind museum collections include Mieke Bal's detailed discussion of the American Museum of Natural History, 'Telling, Showing, Showing Off' (1992), Tony Bennett's extensively cited *The Birth of the Museum* (1995) and Pierre Bourdieu and Alain Darbel's *The Love of Art* (1991). More recently, the summer 2010 issue of *Artforum International* addressed the topic 'The Museum Revisited' in twenty-seven short essays by luminaries such as Tino Sehgal and Chantal Mouffe. Barbara Kirschenblatt-Gimblett's *Destination Culture* (1998) remains an inspirational text for its smart and often witty examination of the tourist encounter with the heritage museum. Tracy Davis's 'Performing and the Real Thing in the Postmodern Museum' (1995) and Valerie Casey's 'Staging Meaning' (2005) are important readings of museum culture through a performance studies lens.

More generally, there is extensive inter-disciplinary scholarship about the role of cultural institutions, including theatre and museums, in tourism and especially in the context of cities. Good starting places for engaging with this field are Lily Hoffman et al.'s *Cities and Visitors* (2003), Martin Selby's *Understanding Urban Tourism* (2004) and Chris Rojek and John Urry's *Touring Cultures* (1997). For more focus on theatrical practices and urban environments, see Jen Harvie's *Theatre & the City* (2009) in the same series as this book and D. J. Hopkins et al.'s *Performance and the City* (2009).

There is a substantial body of work devoted to the use of theatrical practice and live interpretation in museum settings. Handbooks include Tessa Bridal's *Exploring Museum Theatre* (2004), Stacy Roth's *Past into Present* (1998) and Catherine Hughes's *Museum Theatre* (1998). Scott Magelssen's *Living History Museums* (2007) provides a terrific analysis of costumed reeanctments designed to give visitors a taste of the past. His book suggests the potential of living history to work against stable interpretation and monovocality, even if many of the museums he studies rarely produce such radical effects. Anthony Jackson and Jenny Kidd's collection *Performing Heritage* (2011) addresses important issues of interpretation, production, participation and impact in the context of museum theatre. The first two chapters of Rebecca Schneider's *Performance Remains* (2011) examine

US Civil War reenactments, in a book that also provides a trenchant analysis of Marina Abramović's practices of re-performance.

For book-length accounts of Abramović's work, readers might explore the catalogue for *Marina Abramović: The Artist Is Present* edited by Klaus Biesenbach (2010), Paula Orrell's *Marina Abramović and the Future of Performance Art* (2010) and James Westcott's *When Marina Abramović Dies* (2010).

Adams, James. 'The Gallery As Theatre, the Artist As Drama Queen.' *Globe and Mail* 19 Jun. 2010: R5.

Alexander, Edward P., and Mary Alexander. *Museums in Motion: An Introduction to the History and Functions of Museums*. 2nd ed. Lanham, MD: AltaMira, 2008.

Andermann, Jens, and Silke Arnold-de Simine. 'Memory, Community, and the New Museum.' *Theory, Culture & Society* 29.1 (2012): 3–13.

Anderson, Gail, ed. *Reinventing the Museum: Historical and Contemporary Perspectives on the Paradigm Shift*. Lanham, MD: AltaMira, 2004.

Ardenne, Paul. 'Marina Abramović: Museum of Modern Art, 14 mars–31 mai 2010.' Trans. L.-S. Torgoff. *Art Press* 368 (2010): 78–79.

Auslander, Philip. *Liveness*. New York and London: Routledge, 1999.

Bal, Mieke. 'Telling, Showing, Showing Off.' *Critical Inquiry* 18.3 (1992): 556–94.

Bennett, Susan. *Theatre Audiences: A Theory of Production and Reception*. 2nd ed. New York and London: Routledge, 1997.

Bennett, Tony. *The Birth of the Museum: History, Theory, Politics*. London and New York: Routledge, 1995.

———. *Pasts beyond Memory: Evolution, Museums, Colonialism*. London and New York: Routledge, 2004.

Benton, Margaret. 'Capturing Performance at London's Theatre Museum.' *Museum International* 194, 49.2 (1997): 25–31.

Biesenbach, Klaus, ed. *Marina Abramović: The Artist Is Present*. Exhibition catalogue with essays by Klaus Biesenbach, Arthur C. Danto,

Chrissie Iles, Nancy Spector, and Jovana Stokić. New York: Museum of Modern Art, 2010.

Birringer, Johannes. 'Dancing in the Museum.' *PAJ* 99 (2011): 44–52.

Bourdieu, Pierre, and Alain Darbel. *The Love of Art: European Art Museums and Their Public.* Cambridge: Polity, 1991.

Bridal, Tessa. *Exploring Museum Theatre.* Walnut Creek, CA: AltaMira, 2004.

Bruce, Chris. 'Spectacle and Democracy: Experience Music Project As a Post-Museum.' *New Museum Theory and Practice: An Introduction.* Ed. Janet Marstine. Oxford: Blackwell, 2006. 129–51.

Casey, Valerie. 'Staging Meaning: Performance in the Modern Museum.' *TDR* 49.3 (2005): 78–95.

Cavendish, Dominic. 'Don't Bring Down the Curtain.' *Daily Telegraph* 22 Mar. 2006. <http://www.telegraph.co.uk/culture/theatre/3651069/Dont-bring-down-the-curtain.html>.

Coffee, Kevin. 'Museums and the Agency of Ideology: Three Recent Examples.' *Curator: The Museum Journal* 49.4 (2006): 435–48.

Connerton, Paul. *How Societies Remember.* Cambridge: Cambridge UP, 1989.

Cotter, Holland. 'Performance Art Preserved, in the Flesh.' *New York Times* 12 Mar. 2010: C25. <http://www.nytimes.com/2010/03/12/arts/design/12abramovic.html?pagewanted=1>.

Davis, Tracy C. 'Performing and the Real Thing in the Postmodern Museum.' *TDR* 39.3 (1995): 15–40.

Discovering the Jewish Museum Berlin. 2nd ed. Berlin: Stiftung Jüdisches Museum, 2005.

Duncan, Carol. 'The Art Museum As Ritual.' *Art Bulletin* 77.1 (1995): 10–13.

Emerling, Jae. 'Marina Abramović: The Artist Is Present: Museum of Modern Art, New York.' *X-TRA* 13.1 (2010): 26–35.

Falk, John H., and Lynn D. Dierking. *The Museum Experience.* 2nd ed. Washington, DC: Whalesback, 1997.

Frater, Sarah. 'Capturing the Art of Performance.' *Wall Street Journal* 24 Apr. 2009. <http://online.wsj.com/article/SB124051401393149093.html>.

Griffin, Tim. 'Many Happy Returns: Interview with Rem Koolhaas.' *Artforum International* 48.10 (2010): 285–91.

————(ed.). 'The Museum Revisited', spec. iss. of *Artforum International* 48.10 (2010).

Grobe, Christopher. 'Twice Real: Marina Abramović and the Performance Archive.' *Theater* 41.1 (2011): 104–13.

HaCohen, Ruth, and Yaron Ezrahi. 'Musing Spaces: Thomas Struth's Poetics of Exposure.' *Thomas Struth: Photographs 1978–2010*. Ed. Anette Kruszynski, Tobia Bezzola, and James Lingwood. New York: Monacelli Press, 2010. 174–80.

Hall, Martin. 'The Reappearance of the Authentic.' *Museum Frictions*. Ed. Ivan Karp, Corinne A. Kratz, Lynn Szwaja, and Tomás Ybarra-Frausto. Durham, NC, and London: Duke UP, 2006. 70–101.

Halpin, Marjorie M. '"Play It Again, Sam": Reflections on a New Museology.' *Museums and their Communities*. Ed. Sheila Watson. London and New York: Routledge, 2007. 47–52.

Hamnett, Chris, and Noam Shoval. 'Museums As Flagships of Urban Development.' *Cities and Visitors: Regulating People, Markets, and City Space*. Ed. Lily M. Hoffman, Susan S. Fainstein, and Dennis R. Judd. Malden, MA: Blackwell, 2003. 219–36.

Harvie, Jen. *Theatre & the City*. Basingstoke, UK: Palgrave Macmillan, 2009.

Hoerig, Karl A. 'Remembering Our Indian School Days: The Boarding School Experience.' *Museum Anthropology* 104.2 (2002), 642–46.

Hoffman, Lily M., Susan S. Fainstein, and Dennis R. Judd. *Cities and Visitors: Regulating People, Markets, and City Space*. Malden, MA: Blackwell, 2003.

Hopkins, D. J., Shelley Orr, and Kim Solga, eds. *Performance and the City*. Basingstoke, UK: Palgrave Macmillan, 2009.

Hughes, Catherine. *Museum Theatre: Communicating with Visitors through Drama*. Portsmouth, NH: Heinemann, 1998.

Jackson, Anthony. 'Engaging the Audience: Negotiating Performance in the Museum.' *Performing Heritage: Research, Practice and Innovation in Museum Theatre and Live Interpretation*. Ed. Anthony Jackson and Jenny Kidd. Manchester: Manchester UP, 2011. 11–25.

Jackson, Anthony, and Jenny Kidd, eds. *Performing Heritage: Research, Practice and Innovation in Museum Theatre and Live Interpretation*. Manchester: Manchester UP, 2011.

Jackson, Shannon. *Social Works: Performing Art, Supporting Publics*. New York: Routledge, 2011.

Kennedy, Dennis. *The Spectator and the Spectacle*. Cambridge: Cambridge UP, 2009.

Kirschenblatt-Gimblett, Barbara. *Destination Culture: Tourism, Museums and Heritage*. Berkeley: U of California P, 1998.

Knelman, Martin. 'AGO Loses $3M on Costly Flop.' *Toronto Star* 5 Oct. 2010. <http://www.thestar.com/entertainment/article/871148--ago-loses-3m-on-costly-flop>.

Landsberg, Alison. *Prosthetic Memory: The Transformation of American Remembrance in the Age of Mass Culture*. New York: Columbia UP, 2004.

Levine, Abigail. 'Marina Abramović's Time: *The Artist Is Present* at the Museum of Modern Art.' *E-Misférica* 7.2. <http://hemi.nyu.edu/hemi/en/e-misferica-72/levine>.

Low, Theodore. 'What Is a Museum?' *Reinventing the Museum: Historical and Contemporary Perspectives on the Paradigm Shift*. Ed. Gail Anderson. Lanham, MD: AltaMira, 2004. 30–43.

MacCannell, Dean. *The Tourist: A New Theory of the Leisure Class*. 2nd ed. Berkeley and Los Angeles: U of California P, 1999.

MacDonald, Sharon, ed. *A Companion to Museum Studies*. Malden, MA: Blackwell, 2006.

Magelssen, Scott. *Living History Museums: Undoing History through Performance*. Lanham, MD: Scarecrow, 2007.

Marowitz, Charles. *Recycling Shakespeare*. London: Macmillan, 1991.

Marstine, Janet, ed. *New Museum Theory and Practice: An Introduction*. Oxford: Blackwell, 2006.

Morgan, Robert C. 'Thoughts on Re-performance, Experience and Archivism.' *PAJ* 96 (2010): 1–15.

Noordegraaf, Julia. *Strategies of Display: Museum Presentation in Nineteenth- and Twentieth-Century Visual Culture*. Rotterdam: NAi, 2004.

Orrell, Paula. *Marina Abramović and the Future of Performance Art*. New York: Prestel, 2010.

Patraka, Vivian M. *Spectacular Suffering: Theatre, Fascism, and the Holocaust*. Bloomington: Indiana UP, 1999.

Pearson, Mike. *Site-Specific Performance*. Basingstoke, UK: Palgrave Macmillan, 2010.

———. *Imperial Eyes: Travel Writing and Transculturation*. London: Routledge, 1992.

Prior, Nick. 'Postmodern Restructurings.' *A Companion to Museum Studies*. Ed. Sharon MacDonald. Malden, MA: Blackwell, 2006. 509–24.

Rancière, Jacques. *The Emancipated Spectator*. London: Verso, 2009.

Reading, Anna. 'Digital Interactivity in Public Memory Institutions: The Uses of New Technologies in Holocaust Museums.' *Media, Culture & Society* 25 (2003): 67–85.

Rojek, Chris, and John Urry, eds. *Touring Cultures: Transformations of Travel and Theory*. London and New York: Routledge, 1997.

Roth, Stacy F. *Past into Present: Effective Techniques for First-Person Historical Interpretation*. Chapel Hill: U of North Carolina P, 1998.

Rothstein, Edward. 'Museum with an American Indian Voice.' *New York Times* 21 Sept. 2004: E1.

Schechner, Richard. *Performance Studies: An Introduction*. 2nd ed. New York and London: Routledge, 2006.

Schneider, Bernhard. *Daniel Libeskind, Jewish Museum Berlin*. 5th ed. Munich: Prestel, 2005.

Schneider, Rebecca. *Performance Remains: Art and War in Times of Theatrical Reenactment*. London: Routledge, 2011.

Selby, Martin. *Understanding Urban Tourism: Image, Culture and Experience*. London and New York: I.B. Tauris, 2004.

Serota, Nicholas. *Experience or Interpretation: The Dilemma of Museums of Modern Art*. London: Thames & Hudson, 2000.

Skramstad, Harold. 'An Agenda for Museums in the Twenty-First Century.' *Reinventing the Museum: Historical and Contemporary Perspectives on the Paradigm Shift*. Ed. Gail Anderson. Lanham, MD: AltaMira, 2004. 118–32.

Smith, Melanie K. *Issues in Cultural Tourism Studies*. London and New York: Routledge, 2003.

Solomon, Alisa. 'The Artist's Present.' *Killing the Buddha* 3 Jun. 2010. <http://killingthebuddha.com/mag/icon/the-artists-present/>.

Taylor, Diana. *The Archive and the Repertoire: Performing Cultural Memory in the Americas*. Durham, NC, and London: Duke UP, 2003.

van den Berg, Klaus. 'Staging a Vanished Community: Daniel Libeskind's Scenography in the Berlin Jewish Museum.' *Performance and the City*. Ed. D. J. Hopkins, Shelley Orr, and Kim Solga. Basingstoke, UK: Palgrave Macmillan, 2009. 222–39.

Volkert, James, Linda R. Martin, and Amy Pickworth. *National Museum of the American Indian*. London: Scala, 2004.

Watson, Sheila, ed. *Museums and Their Communities*. London and New York: Routledge, 2007.

Westcott, James. *When Marina Abramović Dies: A Biography*. Cambridge, MA: MIT Press, 2010.

Wilkinson, Chris. 'Noises Off: Museums Can't Capture the Essence of Theatre.' *Guardian Unlimited* 26 Mar. 2009.

Witcomb, Andrea. *Re-imagining the Museum: Beyond the Mausoleum*. London and New York: Routledge, 2003.

index